Welcome to the Jungle

Everything You Need to Know to Be a Bengals Fan

Mary Schmitt Boyer

TRIUMPH
BOOKS

Library of Congress Cataloging-in-Publication Data

Boyer, Mary Schmitt.
   Welcome to the jungle : everything you need to know to be a Bengals fan / Mary Schmitt Boyer.
        p. cm.
   Includes bibliographical references.
   ISBN-13: 978-1-57243-934-4
   ISBN-10: 1-57243-934-3
   1. Cincinnati Bengals (Football team)—History. I. Title.
   GV875.C556B69 2008
   796.332'640977178—dc22

                                                    2008009232

This book is available in quantity at special discounts for your group or organization. For further information, contact:

   Triumph Books
   542 South Dearborn Street
   Suite 750
   Chicago, Illinois 60605
   (312) 939-3330
   Fax (312) 663-3557

Printed in U.S.A.
ISBN: 978-1-57243-934-4
Design by Patricia Frey
Photos courtesy of Getty Images unless otherwise indicated

Contents

Acknowledgments

First I must thank all those current and former Bengals players and coaches interviewed for this book. For his endless patience, I thank Jack Brennan, the Bengals' public relations director. I also thank Geoff Hobson, editor of bengals.com; Steve Corn, athletic director at Pickens High School in Pickens, South Carolina; Dan Masonson of the NFL Network; and Ruth Robles in Reggie Williams's office at Disney Sports Attractions. Thanks to my bosses and the fine writers at *The* (Cleveland) *Plain Dealer, The Cincinnati Enquirer, The Cincinnati Post,* and the *Dayton Daily News.* Thanks to the *Plain Dealer* News Research department and Mary Ellen Kollar at the Cleveland Public Library. And thanks to Tom Bast at Triumph Books for thinking of me.

The following books were used in researching this one: *PB: The Paul Brown Story,* by Paul Brown with Jack Clary; *Chad: I Can't Be Stopped,* by Paul Daugherty; and *The Legends, Cincinnati Bengals: The Men, the Deeds, the Consequences,* by Chick Ludwig. In addition, much information came from the Bengals' 2006 media guide.

Introduction

It has been a rough couple of years for the Cincinnati Bengals and their fans.

After a thrilling 2005 season, when the Bengals went 11–5 and advanced to the playoffs only to lose to eventual Super Bowl winner Pittsburgh in the wild-card round, Cincinnati fans thought their time had come at last. They couldn't wait for the 2006 season, when many NFL observers predicted a long playoff run and a possible Super Bowl appearance. Many of the team's young stars seemed to be coming into their own, and coach Marvin Lewis, who'd never had a losing season in Cincinnati, was the toast of the town.

When the Bengals went 4–0 in the preseason, it all but confirmed a title run. Then the regular season started. The offense held up its end of the bargain, ranked eighth in the league, but the defense was ranked 30th. Still, the Bengals had a chance to make the playoffs. But Shayne Graham, the second most accurate field-goal kicker in NFL history, missed a 39-yard field goal with 12 seconds left in what became a 23–17 overtime loss to Pittsburgh that cost the team its chance to advance to the postseason. In a sad reflection of the defensive problems that plagued the team all season, on the third play of the overtime period, Pittsburgh quarterback Ben Roethlisberger threw a short pass to Santonio Holmes, who turned it into a 67-yard game-winning touchdown. The Bengals finished 8–8, so Lewis's streak was alive. It wasn't exactly the ending he'd been hoping for, but he'd still never had a losing season in his four years at the helm.

Then came 2007. The team struggled to a 7–9 record, and only a two-game winning streak at the end of the year allowed the Bengals to reach that level. The offense ranked 11th overall in scoring and 10th in yards per game, but the defense ranked 24th in points allowed and 27th in yards allowed.

In addition, the team was plagued by the irresponsible actions of its players away from the field, becoming the poster child for bad behavior by professional athletes, and the punch line for jokes by the nation's pundits.

That was not what Bengals fans, or their embarrassed and outraged coach, had in mind.

A struggling 2007 season and player problems did not make coach Marvin Lewis a happy man.

In frustration at the end of the year, some of the team's biggest stars spoke out. Quarterback Carson Palmer suggested that changes in the position coaches might be necessary if the team was going to rebound. Wide receiver Chad Johnson, feeling unappreciated, asked to be traded. Even Lewis suggested that the team might need to be blown up, though he later softened that stance a bit.

"Don't take the extreme word I used," he said, speaking to reporters at the end of the season. "But things have to change. It's the end of a football season, and it's inevitable that changes occur. We need to start from anew. There have to be revisions to things we do, and [we] need to understand that there has to be urgency. What happens a lot in coaching is that you kind of just continue on, and you get stale. We have to find a better way. I have to take critical looks at things."

Asked what identity he wanted his team to have, Lewis told reporters, "We need to be a physical football team. If we're not, we're going to struggle week-in and week-out. We're always going to be able to throw the football. We have a fine, outstanding quarterback. We have to be able to run the football effectively to take pressure off him. We have to defend the run effectively and not allow explosive plays. You have to win your third downs. If you do those things, you'll be successful. We had 14 turnovers in the first five games, and you can't do that. You're putting yourself in jeopardy of not being very good. You might end up being 1–4 if you have 14 turnovers after five games, because you can't overcome that. Those things led us to where we are today. We didn't strap a couple of wins back-to-back to get out of that funk."

So the Bengals entered the 2008 off-season with much work to do. They started with some coaching changes, naming Mike Zimmer defensive coordinator and Jeff FitzGerald linebackers coach. They found positives where they could, whether it was signing free agent defensive end Antwan Odom, or the return of troubled linebacker

Odell Thurman after a two-year suspension by NFL Commissioner Roger Goodell for a DUI arrest in 2006.

Palmer and Johnson continue to anchor the Bengals' potent offense, while the changes on the defensive side of the coaching staff were aimed to correct the problems on that side of the ball. Devoted fans continue to hope, as they have for so many years, that the team will get it together and mount a serious bid for its first trip to the Super Bowl since 1988.

If there is one thing that has remained constant throughout Bengals history, it is the passion of the fans who fill Paul Brown Stadium week after week, rain or shine, in heat waves and cold snaps. The team's history is short in comparison to some NFL franchises, but it has been filled with pride and promise since the legendary Paul Brown founded the team and put his distinctive stamp on it. A visit to the stadium bearing his name remains a unique experience in professional football for the longtime season-ticket holder or the newcomer to the Queen City.

As they say to friend and foe alike: Welcome to the Jungle.

Chapter One

Pro Football in Cincinnati

Pro football had some fits and starts before it finally caught on in Cincinnati.

The first pro football team was the Cincinnati Celts, part of the American Professional Football Association, the precursor to the National Football League. In the only year of their existence, the Celts compiled a 1–3 record in the league's second season, 1921.

Twelve years later, the NFL awarded Cincinnati another team, this time called the Reds. That team lasted two seasons. It finished 3–6–1 in 1933 and started 0–8 in 1934 before folding its tents. The independent St. Louis Gunners bought the Cincinnati franchise and went 1–2 in the last three weeks of that season.

For the next several years, it was the American Football League, rather than the Cincinnati franchise, that couldn't survive.

In 1937, the new Bengals—the team from which the modern-day team drew its nickname—went 2–4–2, but the league folded after that season. The same thing happened in 1939, when the team finished in second place with a 6–2 record, only to have the league disband again after that season.

Undaunted, the Bengals joined another new AFL in 1940, going 1–7 that season and 1–5–2 the next. Once again the league folded, in part because of the loss of so many players to World War II, and this time the team did, too.

It would be 26 years before the city was ready to try again, and this time they got it right.

After the legendary Paul Brown was fired by Cleveland Browns owner Art Modell in 1963, he and his wife, Katy, moved to La Jolla, California, where they tried to enjoy a life of leisure. Everything should have been perfect, except for one thing: Brown really missed coaching football.

His son Mike put together a study of possible expansion sites, and Cincinnati came out at the top of his list. Before long, Paul Brown was putting together an ownership group and hoping to be awarded

TRIVIA

When did the Bengals introduce their striped helmets?

Answers to the trivia questions are on pages 187–189.

an expansion franchise in the National Football League. But the NFL decided to move into the New Orleans market instead, so in May of 1967, Brown and his group agreed to join the American Football League, knowing that a merger of the two leagues was just around the corner. In his autobiography, *PB: The Paul Brown Story*, Paul Brown credits Jim Rhodes, then–governor of Ohio, Cincinnati mayor Gene Ruehlmann, and *Cincinnati Enquirer* publisher at the time, Francis Dale, with helping secure the franchise for the city.

Of course there were some obstacles, the largest of which concerned a place to play. NFL rules at the time required each team to have a stadium that could seat 50,000. The Reds were playing in

Paul Brown founded the Cincinnati Bengals in 1967 and coached the Bengals to two playoff seasons before retiring in 1975. Brown is considered by many as the father of modern football.

Crosley Field, which held fewer than 30,000 fans. Their owner, Bill DeWitt, didn't want any part of a new downtown stadium. Undaunted, the Bengals ownership group put together a second group to buy the Reds. With two teams to play in the new stadium, the legal barriers began to fall and plans went ahead for Riverfront Stadium to open in 1970. In the meantime, the Bengals would play at the University of Cincinnati's Nippert Stadium for two seasons.

With that hurdle out of the way, Brown—who was elected to the Pro Football Hall of Fame in 1967—went about putting together his second pro football franchise, from coaches to administrators and from secretaries to telephone operators. From his little office on the 18th floor of Carew Tower, Brown called professionals he'd come to know from his many years in football, including a couple who'd

DID YOU KNOW...

That when fans were surveyed for a nickname for the Cincinnati AFL franchise, "Buckeyes" was the most popular choice? Paul Brown vetoed the idea because he did not want the team to be confused with the one from Ohio State University.

worked for the Browns but were no longer employed by the team. When it came time to select a name, Brown headed a committee of three owners, the other two of whom had attended Princeton, whose sports team was the Tigers. (The fact that Brown had attended and later coached at Washington High School, whose team was also nick-named the Tigers, undoubtedly didn't hurt.)

Brown wanted to jazz up "Tigers," though, so he tweaked the nickname to "Bengals"; selected black, orange, and white as the team colors (not to be confused with the brown, orange, and white from that team up north); and designed a neat, but rather plain, uniform.

Then it was time to acquire some players. Technically, they already had a quarterback. They had traded two draft picks to Miami for quarterback John Stofa late in 1967. In 1968, they were awarded 40 picks in the allocation draft, which netted such veterans as Bobby Hunt and Sherrill Headrick. Then they had 41 picks in the 1968 college draft, starting with center Bob Johnson of Tennessee. The Bengals also picked running back Paul Robinson of Arizona in the third round and tight end Bob Trumpy of Utah in the 12th round. All three rookies made the AFL All-Star Game that year. Robinson would lead the league in rushing with 1,023 yards and be named Rookie of the Year.

But they were just faces in the crowd of more than 100 players who turned up for the steamy opening of the Bengals' training camp at Wilmington College in Ohio, about 60 miles northeast of Cincinnati. Little by little, Brown whittled down his roster and the inaugural Bengals team came together.

They would lose their first three preseason games, although in his autobiography Brown recalls a touching moment in the first game, against Kansas City, when the Cincinnati fans stood to sincerely cheer the team's first first down, which didn't come until the third quarter. The baby Bengals would win their last two preseason games against Pittsburgh at Morgantown, West Virginia, and against the New York Jets in Memphis.

"Those final two victories were big moments," Brown wrote in his autobiography, "because we had proved that this untried group of young men had a chance to be successful, and it helped them believe in themselves. The next step was to apply all that we had learned and endured to our first season of play, and though we were no threat for the championship in 1968, I never doubted for a moment that we would ultimately become contenders. There were fence-sitters around the nation who weren't as sure and said perhaps I had made a mistake by coming back to the game. For the next eight seasons, I was very happy to accept that challenge."

Brown was right on all fronts. The Bengals were no threat in 1968. After an opening loss at San Diego, they did win their first two home games to start the season 2–1, but then finished the season 3–11. Still, it took them just three years to qualify for the playoffs, at the time the quickest any expansion team had done so. In fact, a photograph of Brown being carried off the field by his players after clinching that playoff berth adorns the cover of his autobiography.

Brown took the Bengals to the playoffs in 1973 and 1975 before retiring as coach. He remained as general manager and built the teams that reached the Super Bowl under coach Forrest Gregg after the 1981 season and under coach Sam Wyche after the 1988 season. They lost to the San Francisco 49ers both times.

Brown passed away in 1991, and it would be 14 seasons before the Bengals had another winning season. After a decade of frustration, turmoil, and even embarrassment, the Bengals went 11–5 in 2005 under third-year coach Marvin Lewis.

Although the team lost its final three games to finish 8–8 and miss the playoffs in 2006, followed with a 7–9 mark in 2007, the Bengals remain optimistic. With a popular coach like Lewis, talented players such as quarterback Carson Palmer, wide receiver Chad Johnson, and running back Rudi Johnson, and a stout defense led by Pro Bowl cornerback Deltha O'Neal, and rising free safety Madieu Williams, Cincinnati fans are hoping the success Brown envisioned will finally come to pass. It would be a fitting legacy for the founder of the franchise and the namesake of the team's spanking-new stadium, which opened in 2000.

The Father of the Franchise

Marvin Lewis never met Paul Brown, the Cincinnati Bengals founder, who died in 1991. But everywhere Lewis looks, Brown's spirit remains.

The Bengals play in Paul Brown Stadium. Their address is One Paul Brown Stadium. Brown's sons, Mike and Pete, are still involved with the team, as are his grandchildren Katie Blackburn and Paul Brown.

"No question Paul's stamp is still here," Lewis said. "Since I became the head coach, we've really tried to bring in a lot of the sayings and the things he stood for and make them a part of our building and our weight room and our players' wing and our coaches' wing so that we paid him the respect and the attention he was due."

There may not be a more revered sports figure in the state of Ohio than Paul Brown. He didn't invent football, but he revolutionized the sport. He was responsible for founding both of the state's pro

DID YOU KNOW...

That the Brown family originally spelled its name *Browne*? The *e* disappeared somewhere along the way, according to Brown's autobiography, *PB: The Paul Brown Story*.

football franchises—the Bengals and the Browns—and it is only fitting that he has been enshrined in the Pro Football Hall of Fame in Canton, which sits more or less halfway between the two of them.

Brown was born on September 7, 1908, in Norwalk, Ohio, a small town about an hour west of Cleveland. His father, Lester, was a dispatcher for the Wheeling & Lake Erie Railroad. His mother, Ida, was a homemaker. Brown always said he got his disciplined nature from his father and his competitive nature from his mother, who loved nothing better than a good game of cards.

Life in Norwalk was a slice of Americana. Brown and his sister, Marian, could go fishing on their grandfather's farm or listen to a band concert in the park on a Saturday. When Brown was still a boy, his father was transferred to Massillon, Ohio, a city about 75 miles south of Cleveland. At the time, it was a fairly well-to-do steel town with a strong work ethic.

The young Brown was a good athlete who played all sports, but he loved football the best. He got his first football at the age of six, and from then on it was the driving force in his professional life. Although he weighed just 120 pounds, he made the team at Massillon High School as a sophomore, and his first pass went for a touchdown. In addition to football, he played basketball and baseball and competed in the pole vault and long jump in track and field while in high school.

Brown enrolled at Ohio State University, but at 145 pounds, the coaches there told him he was too small to play football. He lasted

Bengals coach and founder Paul Brown used innovative techniques to improve his team, including being the first to use film to study players and opponents on the field.

one year and then, seeking a smaller school, he transferred to Miami University in Oxford, Ohio, where he would become part of its "Cradle of Coaches," including Woody Hayes, Weeb Ewbank, Paul Dietzel, Sid Gillman, Red Blaik, and Walter Alston, all of whom played or coached at the school.

Brown played quarterback, running back, punter, and punt returner for Miami. He also played on the baseball team and managed the Delta Kappa Epsilon fraternity house. Before his college career was over, he'd married his high school sweetheart Katy Kester, and later had three sons Robin, Mike, and Pete.

Although his father had hoped Brown would become a lawyer, coaching was his true calling. His first job was at Severn Prep, a prep school for the Naval Academy. Brown taught English and history and coached football, lacrosse, and track and field. After his football team went 16–1–1 in two seasons, Brown was hired at his alma mater, Washington High School in Massillon. The program had slipped since Brown was in high school, but Brown built it into one of the premier athletic programs in the state, if not the country. In nine seasons, the Tigers went 80–8–2 and won six state titles and four national championships. So strong was Brown's influence that the fans built a 21,000-seat stadium and named it after him. It is still in use today and hosts some of the Ohio high school state championship games.

In 1941, Brown became the head coach at Ohio State, a position he referred to as his ultimate dream. The Buckeyes went 6–1–1 in his first season and 9–1 in his second, winning the 1942 national championship. In 1943, a number of Ohio State players were called to military service for World War II, and the Buckeyes slipped to 3–6. Brown was commissioned as a naval officer and sent to the Great Lakes Naval Training Center outside Chicago, where he coached the football team to a 15–5–2 record in two seasons.

As luck would have it, the All-America Football Conference was being formed as Brown's military commitment was coming to an end, and Arthur "Mickey" McBride hired Brown to be the first coach of the Cleveland team that would bear his name. It would mark the start of an almost unprecedented run of success. The Browns swept through the AAFC, losing just four games in four seasons and winning the title in each of those seasons. In fact, they were so dominant that the AAFC folded and the Browns joined the National Football League in 1950, reaching the championship game in each of their first six seasons and winning the title in 1950, 1954, and 1955.

In addition to being a strict disciplinarian and a fine tactician, Brown was also an innovator. He designed the first face mask, created the first playbook, and ran the first draw play and the first flea flicker. He was the first coach to hire a full-time staff and a scouting department

Paul Brown's Year-by-Year Regular-Season Record in Pro Football

Year	Record	Year	Record	Year	Record
1946	12–2*	1955	9–2–1*	1969	4–9–1
1947	12–1–1*	1956	5–7	1970	8–6
1948	14–0*	1957	9–2–1	1971	4–10
1949	9–1–2*	1958	9–3	1972	8–6
1950	10–2*	1959	7–5	1973	10–4
1951	11–1	1960	8–3–1	1974	7–7
1952	8–4	1961	8–5–1	1975	11–3
1953	11–1	1962	7–6–1		
1954	9–3*	1968	3–11		* won championship

and the first to analyze film. He was the first coach to call plays from the sidelines and shuttle them in by substituting players. He was the first to test the intelligence of players before drafting them and the first to time them in the 40-yard dash. He was also an advocate of equal rights, and his first Cleveland team featured two of the first African Americans in pro football—Marion Motley and Bill Willis.

In Cleveland, Brown compiled a 167–53–8 record, a .750 winning percentage, with one losing season. Still, after Art Modell bought the team in 1961, he fired Brown in 1963. Four years later, Brown was inducted into the Hall of Fame, the same year he was awarded an expansion franchise in the American Football League.

Brown named the team the Cincinnati Bengals after one of the city's former AFL teams. He coached the team in its first eight seasons, compiling a 55–59–1 record and taking the team to the playoffs in 1970, 1973, and 1975. At the time, no other team had made it to the playoffs so early in its history. He retired as coach before the 1976 season.

"I simply felt that it was the proper time to step down," he wrote in his autobiography. "It was an easy decision because I made it myself, I had nothing more to prove, and I wanted to go out on a successful note."

Brown continued as the Bengals' general manager until his death from pneumonia on August 5, 1991. He was 82. He had lived long enough to see the team he founded make the Super Bowl after the 1981 and 1988 seasons, although they lost both games to the San Francisco 49ers.

In his autobiography, he wrote of the guiding principles that led to the success of his teams: "My basic philosophy, the one I have stressed with every team I have ever coached, is simple: everything we do must be in terms of our team and of doing our best. Obviously, the teams were convinced of its appropriateness because our record speaks for itself.…

"The one key reason for our success was this: I always believed that football was just as much a 'people business' as an exact science of plays and formations. Contrary to some misguided public perceptions of me as the taskmaster who treated players like automatons, I worked harder at every phase of the 'people business' than at anything else, from the first time I ever looked at a player in junior high school until the final day I coached the Cincinnati Bengals."

He also wrote that he had no regrets about stepping down when he did: "I have not regretted the decision because I am well satisfied with my 45 years as a coach. I can look back and feel that I never worked a day in my life because what I did wasn't work—it was fun. And as I look back over those many years, I find that no matter how people and times have changed, the words of Dean Elizabeth Hamilton of Miami University still ring true: 'The eternal verities will always prevail. Such things as truth, honesty, character, and loyalty will never change.' I have tried to live my whole life by those words—and it has made me a happy man."

The Field Generals

Since the franchise began playing in 1968, the Bengals have had only nine head coaches. That means their coaches have served an average of 4.4 seasons. Founder Paul Brown and Sam Wyche served the longest, at eight seasons apiece. Homer Rice had the shortest tenure, at 27 games. Until they reached out to hire Marvin Lewis from the staff of the Washington Redskins before the 2003 season, the Bengals had a history of selecting coaches who had a previous tenure with the team—either as players or as coaches. In that sense, Brown and his son, current Bengals president Mike Brown, kept things in the "family" they had created. The only other exception besides Lewis was Forrest Gregg, who had been an assistant coach and a head coach with the Cleveland Browns before the Bengals hired him in 1980. Of course, since Paul Brown had founded the Browns, too, that almost counts, although Gregg and Paul Brown were not with Cleveland at the same time.

Here's a brief look at the men who have been head coaches with the Bengals. Some of them are examined in greater detail in other chapters.

Paul Brown, 1968–75: 55–59–1. Some men are fortunate enough to build one team from the ground up. Brown got to build two—the Browns and the Bengals. There was no detail in either franchise that escaped his eye. He had the final say on every decision from quarterbacks to socks, and he almost always made the right call on all of them. He built his reputation as a master innovator with the Browns, and enjoyed his greatest on-the-field success in Cleveland, going 167–53–8 in the All-America Football Conference and the NFL from 1946 to 1962, and winning seven titles in 10 years.

After being summarily dismissed by new owner Art Modell after the 1962 season, Brown got a chance to start over in Cincinnati, and he brought the same passion to the Bengals. After an 11–3 season in 1975, which ended with a 31–28 loss at Oakland in the first round of the playoffs, Brown surprised everybody by resigning as coach on New Year's Day 1976. He continued in his role as general manager until his death at the age of 82 on August 5, 1991.

Bill Johnson, 1976–78: 18–15–0. William Levi Johnson Sr., born on July 14, 1926, in Tyler, Texas, was Brown's handpicked successor. "I felt he shared my general coaching beliefs, even though he apparently felt otherwise about some of them," Brown wrote in his autobiography. Johnson, whose nickname was Tiger, had played football at Tyler Junior College and Stephen F. Austin State University before a nine-year career at center for the San Francisco 49ers, from 1948 to 1956. Brown had brought him aboard as the Bengals offensive line coach when the franchise began play in 1968. In Johnson's first season as head coach, the Bengals finished a respectable 10–4. In his second season, they were 8–6. A loss to Houston in the season finale cost them a spot in the playoffs. But when quarterback Ken Anderson broke a bone in his hand and missed the first four games, the team started the 1978 season 0–5, and Johnson resigned. From 1985 to 1990, he coached the Bengals tight ends for Sam Wyche.

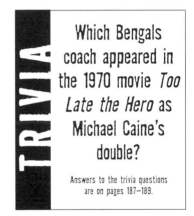

TRIVIA

Which Bengals coach appeared in the 1970 movie *Too Late the Hero* as Michael Caine's double?

Answers to the trivia questions are on pages 187–189.

Homer Rice, 1978–79: 8–19–0. Rice, who'd been brought in to coach the Bengals quarterbacks in 1978, took over that 0–5 team and the Bengals went 4–7 the rest of the way. In his 1979 autobiography, Brown wrote, "Homer has done a superlative job of putting the pieces back together, but in fairness to Bill, injuries at key positions had been disastrous." Things did not improve appreciably, however, and after a 4–12 season in 1979, Rice returned to the college ranks, where he enjoyed considerable renown.

DID YOU KNOW...

That Bill "Tiger" Johnson is the father of William R. Johnson—president, CEO, and chairman of H.J. Heinz? William Johnson says his father gave him his competitive spirit and will to win.

Born February 20, 1927, Rice was a former high school football coach with a Ph.D. from Centre College in Danville, Kentucky. He also coached college teams at Kentucky, Oklahoma, Cincinnati, and Rice University. Before joining the Bengals, he was the athletics director at the University of North Carolina from 1969 to 1975 and Rice University from 1976 to 1977. After leaving the Bengals, he became athletics director at Georgia Tech from 1980 to 1997, where he developed a program later adopted by the NCAA to help athletes succeed not just in sports, but in academics and general life. The NCAA Division IA Athletic Directors present the Homer Rice Award to a former Division IA athletics director for his or her contributions to intercollegiate athletics.

Forrest Gregg, 1980–83: 34–27–0. Gregg is that rarest of NFL coaches who actually might have been better known as a player. That might be the norm in the NBA, but it doesn't happen too often in the NFL. Gregg, born October 18, 1933, in Birthright, Texas, was inducted into the Pro Football Hall of Fame as an offensive tackle after winning six championships, five with the Green Bay Packers and one with the Dallas Cowboys. He played in 188 straight games, was named an All-NFL player eight times, and earned nine Pro Bowl nods.

Gregg started his coaching career as an assistant in San Diego in 1973 and moved to Cleveland as an assistant in 1974. He coached the Cleveland Browns from 1975 to 1977 before joining the Bengals in 1980. He led Cincinnati to Super Bowl XVI after the 1981 season, where they lost to the San Francisco 49ers, 26–21. He left the Bengals in 1983 and coached the Packers from 1984 to 1987. His NFL coaching record was 75–85–2, and he was 2–2 in the playoffs. He also coached the Canadian Football League's Toronto Argonauts in 1979 and Shreveport Pirates in 1994–95. His CFL coaching record was 13–39.

Gregg served as the Ottawa Renegades' vice president of football operations in 2005 before retiring to Colorado Springs. Between CFL stints, he coached at his alma mater, Southern Methodist University, in 1989–90, when it came off the "death penalty" imposed by the NCAA after serious violations. Gregg was 3–19 as the SMU coach and served as the athletics director from 1990 to 1994.

Sam Wyche, 1984–91: 64–68–0. Wyche was a former Bengals quarterback who became the Bengals' most colorful coach. Born January 5, 1945, in Atlanta, Wyche played at Furman University and with Wheeling in the Continental Football League before a seven-year NFL playing career that also included stops in Washington, Detroit, and St. Louis. He started his coaching career in 1979 with the San Francisco 49ers under Bill Walsh, who'd been his mentor as a player in Cincinnati. After one year as the head coach at Indiana University in 1983, he rejoined the Bengals in 1984, leading them to Super Bowl XXIII after the 1988 season, when they lost to Walsh and the San Francisco 49ers, 20–16. Wyche left the Bengals after the 1991 season and was the head coach of the Tampa Bay Buccaneers from 1992 to 1995.

Wyche then began a lucrative career in broadcasting and public speaking, but his new career was interrupted when his left vocal cord was severed during a biopsy on his lymph nodes in 2000. He acted as the Buffalo Bills' quarterbacks coach in 2004–05 and also volunteered at Pickens High School near his home in South Carolina. By 2006, his voice had healed enough that he was able to resume his broadcasting career.

Dave Shula, 1992–96: 19–52–0. Shula is the son of Hall of Fame coach Don Shula. Born May 28, 1959, in Lexington, Kentucky, his NFL playing career consisted of one season with the Baltimore Colts, where he was a wide receiver and kickoff returner in 1981. In 1982, he joined his father's coaching staff in Miami. Shula became offensive coordinator for the Dallas Cowboys in 1989 and joined the Bengals as an assistant in 1991. A year later, at the age of 32, he became one of the youngest head coaches in NFL history. Unfortunately, his career was considerably shorter and much less successful than his father's— he was fired when the team started 1–6 in 1996. After leaving the Bengals, Shula joined his family's steakhouse business.

Bruce Coslet, 1996–2000: 21–39–0. Coslet was also a former Bengals player, a tight end from 1969 to 1976. He was Wyche's offensive coordinator before leaving to become head coach of the New York Jets from 1990 to 1993. The Bengals hired Coslet back as offensive coordinator before promoting him when Shula was fired, as the 1996 team started 1–6. The Bengals went 7–2 the rest of that season, 7–9 in 1997, 3–13 in 1998, and 4–12 in 1999. Coslet resigned after the Bengals started the 2000 season 0–3. Born August 5, 1946, in Oakdale, California, Coslet played at College of the Pacific. When he left Cincinnati, Dallas coach Dave Campo hired him as the Dallas Cowboys offensive coordinator from 2002 to 2003 before Bill Parcells replaced Campo. Coslet is now retired and living in Florida.

Dick LeBeau, 2000–02: 12–33–0. LeBeau is the only other Ohio native besides Brown to act as Bengals head coach. Born September 9, 1937, in London, Ohio, he attended Ohio State, where he played cornerback and halfback for the legendary Woody Hayes and won a national championship in 1957. He played 14 years as a defensive back with the Detroit Lions, making the Pro Bowl from 1965 to 1967. He holds the NFL record for consecutive-game appearances for a cornerback, with 171.

LeBeau was an assistant coach with the Bengals from 1980 to 1991 and again from 1997 to 1999; he was promoted to head coach when Bruce Coslet resigned after losing the first three games in 2000. Although his tenure as the Bengals' head coach was unimpressive, LeBeau has been much in demand as an assistant after designing the zone blitz defense. He was an assistant with Philadelphia and Green Bay before coming to Cincinnati, and he worked for Pittsburgh and Buffalo afterward. He is currently the defensive coordinator for the Steelers team that won the Super Bowl after the 2005 season.

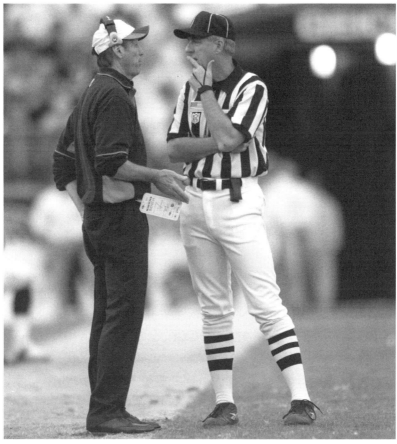

Though he has enjoyed great success as a defensive assistant, Dick LeBeau's tenure as the Bengals head coach was short and disappointing.

Former Bengals safety turned broadcaster Solomon Wilcots is one of LeBeau's biggest fans.

"He's a genius coordinator," Wilcots said. "He should be a Hall of Fame player. When he retired he was second on the all-time list, behind his teammate Dick 'Night Train' Lane, in career interceptions [with 62]. In his 14-year career as a cornerback with the Detroit Lions, he played with Lem Barney and 'Night Train' Lane…. The day you hit 60 interceptions, you go straight to the Hall of Fame. You get 50, you go. Those other two guys are in the Hall of Fame. He should be there.

"The zone blitz scheme still confuses the best quarterbacks. It's what [New England coach] Bill Belichick has used and been labeled a genius. That started with Dick LeBeau. He is the architect of the zone blitz scheme. Bill Belichick will tell you that. It confounds the offensive line and the quarterback simultaneously. It turns defense into an offensive game on third down. The defenses that use that scheme score more touchdowns…. They play with an offensive mentality. They look forward to getting a team to third-and-long so they know it's time to make a big play.

"Over the 86-year history of our league, he's been in it for 40, and he has impacted this game greatly."

Marvin Lewis, 2003–Present: 42–39–0. Bengals founder Brown never met Lewis. But as a noted proponent of affirmative action, Brown would have been thrilled that the team had hired its first African American coach. Lewis brought impressive credentials from the college and pro ranks, including a Super Bowl ring from the Baltimore Ravens, where he directed the team's record-setting defense. Born September 23, 1958, in McDonald, Pennsylvania, outside Pittsburgh, he was no stranger to hard work, having watched his father toil in the steel industry and even spending a summer there himself in college. As hard as he works at improving his football team, Lewis works just as hard to make himself a part of the Cincinnati community.

Chapter Two

Clothes Make the Men

Ever heard that old saying, "A leopard doesn't change its spots?"

Not so for a tiger. In fact, nothing could be further from the truth as far as the Bengals are concerned. The team's uniforms and helmets have undergone frequent changes, as has the logo used on them. The Bengals' distinctive striped helmet has become so readily identifiable that with just a glimpse it's easy to determine who is playing. Like the Packers' football-shaped "G" or the Colts' horseshoe, the striped helmet has become the enduring symbol of the Bengals.

The ironic thing is that although Paul Brown was the general manager of the Bengals and approved the striped helmet as part of a uniform change before the 1981 season, it was contrary to everything he had believed about uniforms.

In his autobiography, *PB: The Paul Brown Story*, Brown wrote, "I was also involved in designing our uniforms as I had done at Cleveland. My one key principle was 'nothing too flashy' because nothing is worse than a bad team with a crazy-looking uniform. The old Denver Broncos' vertical-striped stockings had made them a laughingstock in the early sixties, and I was determined to avoid anything that might bring ridicule while we struggled to become respectable. I know that many people have said I patterned the Bengals' uniform and colors after the Browns, but that is not so. In addition to our helmets being different, our orange, black, and white colors are representative of our symbol, the Bengal tiger; the Browns' colors are orange, brown, and white."

TRIVIA

Before black pants were added as an official part of the uniform in 2004, how many times had the Bengals worn black pants?

Answers to the trivia questions are on pages 187–189.

In an article in the Bengals game program on September 18, 1994, Jack Clary wrote that Brown shunned 25 ideas for the Bengals' uniforms before finally designing one himself. Clary also wrote that Brown got 50 different designs for the helmet, thanks to a class project assigned by a University of Cincinnati professor of fashion design.

Former Bengals business manager John Murdough told Clary, "There were tigers everywhere…helmets with little tigers on the front, tigers on the side, jumping tigers, one with a big open tiger mouth. We got one that was totally black with the word 'Bengals' written on the side. We had another with 'Bengals' written on the front. There was one covered with little footballs and another with a jumping tiger carrying a football in his mouth. We even got one that had written on the side: 'Get your season tickets now,' and another that said 'For Bengals information call 621-3550.'"

Brown took charge again and patterned the stripes on the helmet after those on the head of the tiger-skin rug in his office.

Mind you, the new striped helmets made their debut in 1981, after the Bengals had gone 4–12 in 1978 and 1979 and 6–10 in

1980. Archie Griffin was a running back on those teams, and he recalled the helmets serving as a sort of motivation, although not necessarily in the traditional way.

"We figured we'd better play great football or we were really going to get laughed at," said Griffin, now the president of the Ohio State University Alumni Association.

That's not to say the players were against the change.

"We felt like it was time we had a new logo," Griffin said. "We'd struggled for the past three years, and we thought it was something that would shake us up. The guys took it to heart, and we went out and played like a new team. So it all worked out.

Running back Rudi Johnson shows off the new Bengals uniform, complete with the tell-tale orange and black tiger stripes, in 2004.

DID YOU KNOW...

That there is no league rule requiring uniform numbers on the backs of helmets? The real reason teams use them is so players can readily identify their helmets when they take them off and leave them on the ground or on a bench.

"We looked like new Bengals, and we were."

According to the Bengals' press guide, there are five distinct uniform periods and five different logos, though the two don't match up exactly.

The original uniforms were worn from the team's inception in 1968 until 1979. This uniform included an orange helmet with a gray face mask. It had "Bengals" printed in block letters on each side. There were black jerseys and white jerseys, each with an orange stripe surrounded by two black stripes on the sleeves and block letters and numerals. The team wore white pants with either jersey. The pants had an orange stripe surrounded by black stripes down the outside of each leg. For its first seven seasons, the team wore black-topped striped socks with the black jerseys and white-topped striped socks with the white jerseys. But in 1975, the team went to white-topped striped socks exclusively. The team wore black shoes between 1968 and 1973 and then switched to white shoes.

In 1980, the face mask went from gray to black and black uniform numbers were added to the back of the helmets. Uniform numbers were placed on the sleeves of the jersey, just above the stripes. Also, the orange stripe on the side of the pants was widened.

In 1981, the team introduced its bold new uniforms. The striped helmet attracted the most attention, but there were many other changes. The jerseys now featured black tiger stripes on an orange band around the armholes. That same black-striped orange band ran down the outside of the pant legs. The team also wore orange-topped white socks with its white shoes.

That look prevailed for the next 15 seasons, but there were some changes for the 1997 season. The new leaping-tiger logo appeared on the bottom of the jersey sleeves, while the uniform numbers were moved to the top of the sleeves along the shoulder. The black stripes on the orange bands of the jerseys and pants got wider. The socks went from orange-topped to black-topped.

In 2004, the uniform was completely redesigned for just the second time in team history and the first time in 23 years. However, the striped helmets remained. An orange jersey was added, as were black pants. The orange-topped socks returned as an option. Black shoes were back, too. All three jerseys featured wider tiger-striping on the sleeves, and the stripes on the outside of the pants taper to a point above the knees. The new striped *B* logo appears just below the neck-line on the front of the jersey.

The leaping tiger and striped *B* logos were the only two of the five logo designs that have ever been worn on the Bengals' uniforms. The first logo, used during the AFL days, was a cartoonish tiger carrying a football with his helmet flying off. The second logo was an orange helmet with *Bengals* in block letters, which lasted from 1970 to 1980. That was replaced by a striped helmet, which lasted from 1981 to 1996.

Home Sweet Home

Probably the best thing that can be said about the Cincinnati Bengals' first home—Nippert Stadium at the University of Cincinnati—is that the Bengals had to play there only two years, until Riverfront Stadium (renamed Cinergy Field in 1996) was completed.

It's likely no one was sorry to leave Nippert Stadium, where the Bengals went 6–8 from 1968 to 1969.

"Nippert Stadium was awful," former Bengals tight end Bob Trumpy said. "They painted the dirt green. The locker room we eventually ended up using was probably about 75 yards from the field, and you had to go up concrete steps in football spikes. We had some people slip and fall. We played Oakland one time, and I put my hand down on the ground on the first play of the game, which was in late October, and my fingers went into the dirt—it was actually mud— all the way up to the second [knuckle]. As I remember, we had to call a timeout before the first play because several players had that happen.

"But hey, it was the NFL. I don't think we really cared where we played. It was the NFL."

Paul Brown, founder and coach of the Bengals, had a slightly different take on the place, which held about 28,000.

"The two seasons we spent at Nippert were fun," Brown wrote in his autobiography. "I'm even sure that Nippert's limited dressing facilities helped us on more than one occasion. For the first couple of games, we occupied one that was so hot and muggy it simply drained the strength from our players. We subsequently moved up to the university's field house and put the visitors in the steamy dressing room. I think a couple of teams were actually beaten because their players had just wilted in that room even before the game started, while my young, eager beavers were full of energy."

Nippert Stadium served its purpose, though. It gave the Bengals a place to play their first two seasons, which meant history was made there.

In their first preseason game at Nippert, on August 3, 1968, the Bengals lost to the Kansas City Chiefs, 38–14, before a crowd of 21,682. In their first regular-season game on September 15, 1968, they beat the Denver Broncos, 24–10, before a crowd of 25,049. Dale Livingston scored the first points for the Bengals with a 49-yard field goal in the third quarter, and Trumpy scored the first touchdown later in that quarter. The team drew its biggest crowd of 28,642 for a 31–10 loss to San Diego on September 29, 1968. The last game the Bengals played in Nippert Stadium was a 25–14 loss to Boston on November 16, 1969, in front of 25,913 fans.

No wonder Riverfront Stadium felt like a palace when the team moved in for the 1970 season.

"That was a big deal," Trumpy said. "The Cincinnati Reds had already used the stadium for almost their entire season. It was very, very nice."

The Bengals played at Nippert Stadium and Riverfront Stadium/Cinergy Field before finally calling Paul Brown Stadium home, in 2000.

The $50 million circular stadium was similar to stadiums in Pittsburgh and Philadelphia, with four tiers of multicolored seats. It had all the amenities of the times, including Astroturf. A crowd of 52,299 showed up on August 8, 1970, to check it out in the Bengals' 27–12 victory over Washington in the first preseason game, while 56,616 showed up for the first regular-season game, a 31–21 victory over Oakland on September 20, 1970.

Overall, the Bengals went 128–100 in regular-season games at Riverfront Stadium/Cinergy Field. Their biggest crowd was 60,284 for a 27–24 loss to Cleveland on October 17, 1971. In their last game there, a crowd of 59,972 watched the Bengals thump the Browns, 44–28, on December 12, 1999. The Bengals went out with a bang, holding the Browns to an opponent record-low 11 net yards rushing on 11 carries. The Browns' longest run of the day was three yards. Conversely, Cincinnati ran for 279 yards on 53 carries, which was then the second most rushing yards in team history and the most in a home game.

With the Bengals and the Reds sharing a stadium for all those years, by the turn of the century it was showing its age. Like many teams in many towns, each team wanted its own stadium. The $400 million Paul Brown Stadium opened in August of 2000, only a few blocks from the site of the old Riverfront Stadium. Located

DID YOU KNOW...

That Nippert Stadium is named after University of Cincinnati football player Jimmy Nippert, who was spiked in the last game of the 1923 season against Miami, developed blood poisoning, and died? His grandfather, James N. Gamble of Procter & Gamble, donated the funds to complete the horseshoe–shaped structure, and the James Gamble Nippert Memorial Stadium was dedicated on November 8, 1924. It is still in use today.

along the banks of the Ohio River, the 65,500-seat, open-ended stadium offers views of the river and downtown. In 2001, it was the first NFL stadium to receive the Merit Award from the American Institute of Architects (California Council).

Trumpy wishes he could have played there—for more than one reason.

"It's awful nice," he admitted. "They've got the sophisticated Astroturf. I don't know what they call it now. There's several different

TRIVIA

Who was the first player to score for the Bengals in Riverfront Stadium?

Answers to the trivia questions are on pages 187–189.

types. We practiced on Astroturf that was hard as a rock. Then we played on it and that was even harder because the surface at Riverfront Stadium was designed for baseball use, not football use. So it was very, very difficult to play on. I've got bad hips, bad shoulders, a bad back, all from running into people and landing on that Astroturf all the time.

"Certainly, it would be fun to play at Paul Brown Stadium."

The new turf Trumpy referred to is called Field Turf, and it was installed in 2004, replacing the natural grass that had been in place since the stadium opened. Field Turf is more durable than grass and offers more consistent footing. And it is safer for players than other synthetic fields.

The first preseason game was played on August 19, 2000, when 56,180 fans showed up to see the Bengals beat the Chicago Bears, 24–20. A crowd of 64,006 saw the regular-season home opener on September 10, 2000, which the Bengals lost to the Cleveland Browns, 24–7. Ron Dugans scored the first Cincinnati points on a four-yard touchdown pass from Akili Smith with 14:33 left in the second quarter.

The Rallying Cry

Who dey?

If you're a Bengals fan, you don't have to ask. Even if you're not a Bengals fan and you live in Cincinnati, you don't have to ask. The signature phrase from the team's rallying cry is everywhere, and it can mean anything from "hello" to "oh boy" to "Let's go, Bengals." It's the name of the Bengals mascot and part of the name of dozens of businesses, ranging from water taxis to sleigh rides. It's as likely to show up in headlines ("Who Dey Think Gonna Carve a Pumpkin Quite Like This?" in *The Cincinnati Enquirer*) as songs ("Fear Da Tiger" by funkadelic legend Bootsy Collins). At one time, there was Hu-Dey beer, produced by the Hudepohl Brewing Company.

Though there has been much discussion—and no consensus— over its origins, most agree it started during the Bengals' march to their first Super Bowl in the 1981 season. And, much like the team, it has been resurrected recently.

When coach Marvin Lewis arrived in 2003, he saw a video of highlights from the 1988 Super Bowl season, including a clip of the cheer. Lewis asked the leader of the cheer in the video, James Brown of Middletown, to lead the cheer in the team's locker room after victories at Paul Brown Stadium.

"Some teams have a certain tradition that they have in that city or [with] that team," Lewis told *The Cincinnati Enquirer* in 2005. "I thought it was important, something for the guys to have fun with. When you win you ought to enjoy it. It's something to congratulate them for winning and recognition of winning."

Running back Rudi Johnson told *The Enquirer*, "I picked it up as soon as I got here. You can go around here and ask anybody to chant it, and they'll give it to you word for word, line for line. It's a good thing, a good thing to have."

The whole cheer is a question and answer:

"Who dey? Who dey? Who dey think gonna beat dem Bengals?

"Noooooobody!"

Scholarly research indicates the *dey* and *dem* are parts of traditional southern Appalachian dialect brought to Cincinnati by settlers from that area. Local historians claim the genesis of the cheer was an old commercial for Red Frazier Ford that asked, "Who's going to give you a better deal than Red Frazier? Noooooobody."

The biggest question is whether the cheer originated in Cincinnati or New Orleans. The Bengals' first season was 1968. The Saints began a year earlier. At some point, they adopted a cheer: "Who dat? Who dat? Who dat say we gonna beat dem Saints? Nobody."

So which came first, who dey or who dat? Not surprisingly, it depends on who you ask.

The Enquirer found that those with Louisiana ties think the cheer started there. The paper quoted Dr. Joseph Foster, an anthropology professor at the University of Cincinnati who graduated from Louisiana State University, as saying, "I can confirm that this kind of chant in professional football started in New Orleans, or at least was there before [Paul] Brown's football team fans took it up."

Dr. Ray Brassieur, a professor in the department of sociology and anthropology at the University of Louisiana–Lafayette, said he remembered adults repeating a similar line

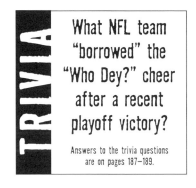

TRIVIA

What NFL team "borrowed" the "Who Dey?" cheer after a recent playoff victory?

Answers to the trivia questions are on pages 187–189.

from a movie. According to the website IMDB.com, the 1976 television movie *Sybil*, starring Sally Field, included the following piece of dialogue between Field and Brad Davis, playing Richard J. Loomis:

Sybil Dorsett: Who dat?

Richard J. Loomis: Who dat who say who dat?

Sybil Dorsett: Who dat who say who dat who say who dat?

DID YOU KNOW...

That as of January 2008, Hu–Dey beer cans were still available on eBay for $1.99 to $9.99?

An article in the *The* (Cleveland) *Plain Dealer* recounted a story about some Saints fans walking into an Irish bar in Cincinnati named Crowley's before a game during the early days of the Bengals. By and by as the drinks flowed, *who dat* became *who dey*.

City councilman David Crowley, whose father opened the bar 70 years ago, told *The Plain Dealer*: "It's about an Irish bar, it's a group of die-hard Bengals fans. There could be a little blarney with that, we maintain a license to do that. Oh yeah, our claim has got as much validity as anything else."

But the most impassioned defense of the cheer's Cincinnati origins is posted on the Bengals' website, www.bengals.com, citing a posting on www.bengalsjungle.com. Not only does bengalsjungle.com refer to the Ford commercial mentioned earlier, but it also contains all the words to a song recorded by a former Cincinnati weatherman:

From the banks of the Ohio comes that orange and black machine
They're the Cincinnati Bengals, the finest ever seen
With stripes upon their helmets and fire in their eyes
They'll take the field, they will not yield
They're strong and tough and wise
Who dey, who dey, who dey think gonna beat them Bengals
Who dey, who dey, who dey think gonna beat them Bengals
Who dey, who dey, who dey think gonna beat them Bengals
Who dey, who dey, who dey think gonna beat them Bengals
Hear that Bengal growling, mean and angry

See that Bengal prowling, lean and hungry
An offensive brute, run, pass, or boot
And defensively, he's rough-errrr tough-errrr
Cincinnati Bengals, that's the team we're gonna cheer to victory
Touchdown Bengals!
Put some points up on the board and win a game for Cincinnati!
Who dey, who dey, who dey think gonna beat them Bengals
Who dey, who dey, who dey think gonna beat them Bengals
Who dey, who dey, who dey think gonna beat them Bengals
Who dey, who dey, who dey think gonna beat them Bengals
Noooooobody

The posting goes on to say the Bengals started the cheer in November 1981, while the Saints' version started in 1983 and became popular again in 1987. So when the Bengals reached the Super Bowl after the 1988 season, many assumed they had taken the cheer from the Saints, who had used it the season before.

Furthermore, the posting says, the first team to use the "Who Dat" cheer was Louisiana State, when it went to the 1982 Orange Bowl against Nebraska. Thus, the posting claims not only did Saints fans not start the cheer, they weren't even the first ones to copy it.

Bonus Babies and Bombs

The National Football League draft, experts like to tell us, is not an exact science. They usually tell us that when defending a draft pick who flopped. Bengals fans have seen far too many of those, much too close together—especially considering how many times the team has had a high pick as the result of a horrible season. But before reviewing some of the draft-day duds, it's worth noting that the team has made some great selections, too. Sometimes all that time and money invested in researching college players actually does pay off. Here are 10 great picks, followed by 10 that weren't so great.

Ten Great Draft Picks

Ken Anderson, quarterback, Augustana College (Illinois), third round, 67th player taken, 1971. Although he had all the skills necessary to play pro football, there was some concern about Anderson because he'd played at such a small school. But knowing that Atlanta coach Norm Van Brocklin was also interested, Bengals coach and general manager Paul Brown, needing a replacement for the injured Greg Cook, pulled the trigger a little earlier than the Bengals had planned. As a result, they wound up with a player who would make four appearances in the Pro Bowl. Brown said in his autobiography, "Ken Anderson ranks just behind Otto Graham as my best quarterback ever." High praise indeed.

Isaac Curtis, wide receiver, San Diego State University, first round, 15th player taken, 1973. Once again, Brown's eye for talent paid off and the Bengals nabbed a world-class sprinter. "Isaac has since become one of the great stars of our era: a big man at 195 pounds, with the grace and balance of a ballet dancer and the hands of Dante Lavelli," Brown wrote in his autobiography.

Boomer Esiason, quarterback, University of Maryland, second round, 38th player taken, 1984. The biggest surprise was that Esiason lasted as long as he did. It didn't take the Bengals long to decide to snap him up when he fell into the second round, where he became the first quarterback selected in that draft. Maybe some scouts were worried about the fact that he was a left-hander, but that hadn't kept him from setting 17 school records for passing and total offense during an All-American career for the Terrapins, who won the Atlantic Coast conference title and a Citrus Bowl berth in 1983.

Bob Johnson, center, University of Tennessee, first round, second player taken, 1968. Johnson, an All-American, had been scouted personally by Brown, who made him the team's first-ever collegiate draft pick. All he did was make the Pro Bowl his first year and play 12 years with the team. "A few people were surprised when we made a center our top pick, but I had thought, 'Well, where do we begin?' and the answer was obvious: since the ball must go from the ground to the quarterback before anything can happen in a game, we might as well start with a center," Brown wrote in his autobiography. "There was more to it than that, though. From meeting him and talking to his coaches, I also knew that Bob was a tremendous person, and he had been a team captain at every level of competition. He was even captain of the College All-Star team that year, and before our first season, I appointed him our offensive captain, a rarity for a rookie. He held the job until his final game as a Bengal, and I never once regretted the choice."

Chad Johnson, wide receiver, Oregon State University, second round, 36th player taken, 2001. Oh, sure, it looks like a slam dunk in hindsight, given the fact that Johnson has blossomed into one of the best wide receivers in the game. But remember, Johnson played only one season of NCAA Division I football and took three seasons to complete a two-year junior college program because he was academically ineligible one season. Although he averaged an eye-popping 21.8 yards per catch in 2000 at Oregon State, he really was an unproven commodity.

Max Montoya, tackle, UCLA, seventh round, 168th player taken, 1979. Any seventh-round pick who makes the Pro Bowl three times

DID YOU KNOW...

That Pete Koch, a first-round pick in 1984 who played just one season in Cincinnati, went on to act in movies and television? He was in *Heartbreak Ridge* with Clint Eastwood and *Heat* with Burt Reynolds, as well as television shows like *Nash Bridges* and *ArliSS*.

for Cincinnati, as Montoya did in 1986, 1988, and 1989, has to qualify as a great draft choice, especially in light of the fact that the Bengals took Jack Thompson in the first round that year. See next section for details.

Anthony Muñoz, tackle, University of Southern California, first round, third player taken, 1980. Although he was an All-American in college, there were questions about his health because he'd already had knee surgery. Thank goodness the Bengals decided not to listen to the doubters. Muñoz played 13 seasons and was selected for the Pro Bowl 11 times, which was a record when he retired in 1992. He became the only Bengals player to be elected to the Pro Football Hall of Fame when he was enshrined in 1998.

Tackle Anthony Muñoz played 13 seasons and was selected for the Pro Bowl 11 times, which was a record when he retired in 1992.

Lemar Parrish, cornerback, Lincoln University (Missouri), seventh round, 163rd player taken, 1970. Seventh-round draft choices aren't even guaranteed to make the team, and seventh-round draft choices from small schools are even more of a risk. This one paid off big-time as Parrish became a fixture in the Bengals defensive back-field—and in the Pro Bowl, with six appearances, second in team history to Anthony Muñoz's 11.

Jess Phillips, defensive back, Michigan State University, fourth round, 84th player taken, 1968. This might qualify as the Bengals' most interesting draft pick. Phillips happened to be in jail for passing bad checks. "We felt, however, that he was basically a good person who had succumbed to some youthful temptation when he had seen some of his former teammates come back to school with plenty of bonus money, flashy clothes, and big cars after a year of professional football," Brown wrote in his autobiography. "My son Mike talked to the prison officials and then to his lawyer, and we were told that if Jess, who was an exemplary prisoner, got a job with us and thus had an opportunity for rehabilitation, he would be released from prison. I had also talked with his coach, Duffy Daugherty, who had told me Jess was a fine boy and a fine football player—good enough to make the All–Big Ten team as a safety in 1967—so we felt we were on safe ground." Phillips started at safety as a rookie, switched to running back the next season, and wound up playing five seasons with the team.

Brown, it must be noted, was one of the first coaches to do this kind of extensive background check on players because character was as important, if not more important, to him as talent. He had to be convinced of Phillips's value because the last thing he would have done was bring in a troublemaker to disrupt the formation of his new franchise.

Bob Trumpy, tight end, University of Utah, 12th round, 301st player taken, 1968. In spite of the fact that 300 players were selected in front of him, Trumpy worked his way into the starting lineup as a rookie; in his first season, he caught 37 passes for 639 yards and earned the first of three straight (and four overall) trips to the Pro Bowl. The best season of his career came in 1969, when he caught 37 passes for 835 yards and nine touchdowns.

Ten Wasted Draft Picks

Ki-Jana Carter, running back, Penn State University, first round, first player taken, 1995. The Bengals wanted Carter so desperately that for the first time, they traded up in the first round to get a player, sending the number five and number 36 picks to Carolina for the number one pick, which they used on the 5'10", 226-pound junior who'd finished second in the 1994 Heisman Trophy race. Unfortunately, Carter suffered a torn anterior cruciate ligament in his left knee in his third preseason game. He missed his entire rookie year and was never the same player after that. Frequently dinged up, he lasted with the Bengals until 1999 and then played sparingly with Washington and New Orleans.

Charles Fisher, cornerback, West Virginia, second round, 33rd player taken. Fisher won the starting left cornerback job his rookie season, but he suffered three torn ligaments in his left knee in the 1999 season opener at Tennessee and never recovered.

Ricky Hunley, linebacker, University of Arizona, first round, seventh player taken, 1984. Hunley was a two-time All-American at Arizona, the first consensus All-American linebacker from the school. But he never came to terms on a contract with the Bengals, who eventually traded him to Denver, where he became a starting linebacker in two Super Bowls. He finally returned to Cincinnati—as linebackers coach—in 2003.

David Klingler, quarterback, University of Houston, first round, sixth player taken, 1992. The defense had been a disaster the previous season, giving up 27 points and 250 yards in passing each game. Everyone figured the Bengals would look to improve on that side of the ball, so taking a quarterback was a surprise, even if Boomer Esiason was getting older. Klingler was 6'3", 210 pounds, and a good athlete, but the Bengals couldn't protect him and he wasn't particularly well-liked. In his two best seasons—1993 and 1994—he threw for 1,935 and 1,327 yards, respectively. But in each of those seasons he threw six touchdowns and nine interceptions, and the Bengals went 3–13. In his four seasons with the team, the Bengals lost almost three-quarters of their games (18–46).

Pete Koch, defensive end, University of Maryland, first round, 16th player taken, 1984. Maybe if the Bengals had to do it all over again, they'd change the order of the players they drafted in 1984 and then things wouldn't look so bad. Ricky Hunley, their first choice in the first round, number seven overall, didn't sign with the team. Koch, their second first-round pick—number 16 overall—lasted just one season with the team before being released. He did play three seasons with Kansas City and another with the Los Angeles Raiders, but a first-round pick has to play more than one season with the team that drafted him or he's got to be considered a flop. Offensive lineman Brian Blados, who was the team's third first-round pick, number 28 overall, did play with the Bengals until 1991. And then there was quarterback Boomer Esiason, the second-round pick who became a star while playing from 1984 to 1992.

Akili Smith, quarterback, University of Oregon, first round, third player taken, 1999. The 1999 draft may go down as one of the weirdest in NFL history. Of the three quarterbacks taken with the first three picks, only Donovan McNabb, who went to the Philadelphia Eagles at number two, developed into the kind of player that justified his selection. Kentucky's Tim Couch was battered for five rough seasons in Cleveland after the Browns opted for him over Smith with the number one selection in 1999.

Smith, who really had only one solid season in college ball, along with some academic and legal problems and a near-miraculous

If Only...

BYU quarterback Steve Young had agreed to join the Bengals in 1984, how might things have been different? The Bengals thought they had a deal worked out for Young as the number one pick in the draft, but instead he opted to sign with the Los Angeles Express of the United States Football League. Thus snubbed, the Bengals traded the number one pick to New England for number 16 pick, Pete Koch, and number 28 pick, Brian Blados.

The Bengals' First-Round Draft Picks

Year	Draft Pick	Player	College	Bengals Career
1968	2	C Bob Johnson	Tennessee	1968–79
1969	5	QB Greg Cook	Cincinnati	1969–74
1970	7	DT Mike Reid	Penn State	1970–74
1971	15	T Vern Holland	Tennessee State	1971–79
1972	2	DE Sherman White	California	1972–75
1973	15	WR Isaac Curtis	San Diego State	1973–84
1974	23	DT Bill Kollar	Montana State	1974–76
1975	14	LB Glenn Cameron	Florida	1975–85
1976	11	WR Billy Brooks	Oklahoma	1976–79
1976	24	RB Archie Griffin	Ohio State	1976–83
1977	3	DT Eddie Edwards	Miami (Florida)	1977–88
1977	8	DT Wilson Whitley	Houston	1977–82
1977	22	TE Mike Cobb	Michigan State	1977
1978	8	DL Ross Browner	Notre Dame	1978–86
1978	16	C Blair Bush	Washington	1978–82
1979	3	QB Jack Thompson	Washington State	1979–82
1979	12	RB Charles Alexander	LSU	1979–85
1980	3	T Anthony Muñoz	USC	1980–92
1981	10	WR David Verser	Kansas	1981–84
1982	26	DE Glen Collins	Mississippi State	1982–85
1983	25	C Dave Rimington	Nebraska	1983–87

1984	7	LB Ricky Hunley	Arizona	Traded
1984	16	DE Pete Koch	Maryland	1984
1984	28	OL Brian Blados	North Carolina	1984–91
1985	13	WR Eddie Brown	Miami (Florida)	1985–91
1985	25	LB Emanuel King	Alabama	1985–88
1986	11	LB Joe Kelly	Washington	1986–89
1986	21	WR Tim McGee	Tennessee	1986–92, 1994–95
1987	17	DE Jason Buck	BYU	1987–90
1988	5	CB Rickey Dixon	Oklahoma	1988–92
1989	None	(traded)		
1990	12	LB James Francis	Baylor	1990–98
1991	18	LB Alfred Williams	Colorado	1991–94
1992	6	QB David Klingler	Houston	1992–95
1992	28	S Darryl Williams	Miami (Florida)	1992–95, 2000–2001
1993	5	DE John Copeland	Alabama	1993–2000
1994	1	DT Dan Wilkinson	Ohio State	1994–97
1995	1	RB Ki-Jana Carter	Penn State	1995–99
1996	10	T Willie Anderson	Auburn	1996–present
1997	14	LB Reinard Wilson	Florida State	1997–2002
1998	13	LB Takeo Spikes	Auburn	1998–2002
1998	17	LB Brian Simmons	North Carolina	1998–2006
1999	3	QB Akili Smith	Oregon	1999–2002
2000	4	WR Peter Warrick	Florida State	2000–2004
2001	4	DE Justin Smith	Missouri	2001–present
2002	10	T Levi Jones	Arizona State	2002–present
2003	1	QB Carson Palmer	USC	2003–present
2004	26	RB Chris Perry	Michigan	2004–2006
2005	17	LB David Pollack	Georgia	2005–2006
2006	24	CB Johnathan Joseph	South Carolina	2006–present
2007	18	CB Leon Hall	Michigan	2007–present

improvement on his Wunderlich score on his second try, had four unimpressive seasons in Cincinnati. He was the starter only in 2000, when he threw for 1,253 yards and three touchdowns for the 4–12 Bengals.

What makes this pick even harder to swallow was New Orleans's willingness to trade all its draft choices to Cincinnati in order to move up to take Ricky Williams. Washington eventually took New Orleans up on its offer.

Jack Thompson, quarterback, Washington State University, first round, third player taken, 1979. Nicknamed "The Throwin' Samoan" in college, Thompson set numerous school, Pac-10, and NCAA records, including 7,818 passing yards, which made him the most prolific passer in NCAA history at the time. But those numbers never translated to success in the pros. The Bengals were hoping to groom him as a successor for Ken Anderson, but in four seasons, Thompson completed just 47.3 percent of his passes with 19 interceptions. The Bengals traded him to Tampa Bay in 1983 for the number one pick in the draft. In true Bengals fashion, however, the team sent that pick to New England for the number 16 and number 28 picks, which they used on Pete Koch, who is included above, and Brian Blados.

TRIVIA

Ki-Jana Carter finished second in the 1994 Heisman Trophy race; who finished first?

Answers to the trivia questions are on pages 187–189.

David Verser, wide receiver, University of Kansas, first round, 10th player taken, 1981. Gaudy statistics but no impact. He averaged 19.7 yards per catch; that was the good news. The bad news was that in 49 games over four seasons, he caught a total of 23 passes for 454 yards and three touchdowns. He held out during his first training camp, which forced Cris Collinsworth into the lineup, so he did have that going for him.

Peter Warrick, wide receiver, Florida State University, first round, fourth player taken, 2000. Okay, he wasn't horrible, and the fact that he wasn't great might have had more to do with the guys who played quarterback during his time with the Bengals. But after becoming a two-time consensus All-American who led Florida State to the national championship games in 1998 and 1999, he wasn't nearly as spectacular as a pro. His best season came in 2003, when he caught a career-high 79 passes for 819 yards and seven touchdowns.

Dan Wilkinson, defensive tackle, Ohio State University, first round, first player taken, 1994. Who knows why some things don't work out? Wilkinson, nicknamed "Big Daddy," was from nearby Dayton and went to Ohio State. He had all the skills and durability for a long career in the NFL. But after signing a $14.4 million contract with the team, he never developed into the player the Bengals had hoped for. He criticized many aspects of the team and called the city racist. He finally forced a trade to the Washington Redskins in 1998. Wilkinson later apologized for the disrespect he'd shown the organization and the city, blaming immaturity.

Chapter Three

A Coach with Credibility

Former Bengals offensive lineman Dave Lapham remembers the first time he met Forrest Gregg. Gregg, a former coach of the Cleveland Browns who had been one of the stars on the Green Bay Packers team that won five NFL titles, was named coach of the Bengals in 1980.

"He got up in front of us at the podium, and he had Super Bowl rings on both of his hands," Lapham recalled. "I said to myself, 'Whoo, that establishes his credibility for me.' He played the position I play, and he went to the pinnacle more than once. He played for Vince Lombardi, and Vince Lombardi was tough on him, so no matter how tough he is on me, I know he did at least that and maybe more. So I bought into it. He had instant credibility with me and a lot of guys on the football team. The fact that his bust was in the Hall of Fame was a motivator.

"He was the most challenging coach I ever played for in terms of pushing you mentally and physically. He had his foot on the gas all the time. He was always pushing for more. I have nothing but respect for him. It was the best football team I ever played on. I can tell you that, easily."

The funny thing is, Gregg had a similar impact on Paul Brown the first time the Bengals founder met him, in 1970. Gregg was still playing with the Packers, who were facing the Bengals in an exhibition game in Milwaukee. He finagled an introduction to Brown before the game.

"I shook hands with Paul, and Paul looked up at me and said, 'You're a big one,'" Gregg said, laughing at the memory.

When Gregg was inducted into the Pro Football Hall of Fame in 1977, Brown was there to induct former Browns star Bill Willis. Gregg got to know Brown better that weekend, and a friendship formed, based on mutual respect.

After Gregg was fired as coach by the Browns in 1977, his phone rang one day. It was Brown.

"He called me and said, 'I think you're a good coach. I'm sorry things didn't work out. I wish you the best of luck,'" Gregg said. "So I felt good about that. Two years later, he called me up when he had an opening and asked if I would be interested. I said, 'I'll be there on the first plane.'"

What was it like working for football legends like Lombardi and Brown?

"I think I was very fortunate," Gregg said. "I played for Vince Lombardi and coached for Paul Brown. I think they were alike in a lot of ways. If you knew Paul Brown and you knew Vince Lombardi, you'd say, 'How were they alike?' Paul was a very innovative guy. He did a lot of things other people are doing in this league right now. He was a disciplinarian, but probably in a different way. Lombardi would scream at you and the next thing you knew, he'd have his arm around you. Paul was more caustic. I never played for him, but I talked to a lot of his players and knew a lot of his players. They would say he would make little short statements if you weren't playing well: 'Just so

Coach Forrest Gregg said of his Super Bowl XVI squad: "I knew at the end of 1980 that this team had great potential."

you know, we're looking at your position in the draft.' That's what I heard from the other players.

"Of all the people I ever knew, Paul Brown had a terrific eye for talent. I think that shows in that first Cleveland Browns team in the old All-America Football Conference. He had some great athletes. When that league folded, he got a lot of players who were in that league. He had firsthand information on those people. That's one way he put a winning team together so quickly. Everybody would like to have that ability and talent, and a lot of people do. But he was unusual.

"Vince Lombardi was the same way about talent. He had a great eye for talent. He was a motivator. If you ask me what his strong suit was, it was being able to motivate players. He had a good system that the players understood, and he made sure they understood it. That's one reason we were successful. Both men were extremely successful."

The Bengals experienced some of their greatest success under Gregg, although not immediately. The 1980 team finished 6–10, but Gregg saw its potential.

"Having coached against that team when I was with the Browns, I knew one thing: I knew there was some talent on that team," Gregg said. "I knew my job would be to make sure these people played up to expectations. I think the timing was right for someone like me to come in there. Some of these guys had played for Paul Brown, so they knew a little bit about discipline, [and] that was one thing I really believed in. My job was to get things in order again. It wasn't that these guys were bad or anything. But I don't care who you are, you've got to know the direction you're going. We put them in the right direction and they responded to it.

"I knew at the end of 1980 that this team had great potential. We didn't win in 1980. We had our ups and downs. But at the end of the season, I felt like we were a football team. At the end of the season, I remember we played Cleveland. We had nothing to play for other than pride. These guys played that game right down to the wire. Pat McInally, our punter who was also a receiver, suffered a mild concussion in that game. I couldn't keep him on the bench. He came back into the ballgame and caught a touchdown pass that put us ahead, right at the end of the game. They came back and scored and beat us. But nevertheless, I thought that was the making of the football team. By that time, Kenny Anderson was starting to arrive."

Anderson, of course, was the quarterback. He was as important to the Bengals as Bart Starr had been to Gregg's Packers.

Asked if the two players were similar, Gregg said, "I don't think any two people are alike.... Kenny Anderson was probably bigger, probably a little better at running than Bart was. Bart was a pocket passer. He knew what was going on on the field and he knew what he was looking for. I'd say Kenny fit that mold, too. He studied the game hard. He had a good arm, had the ability to avoid the rush, and was respected by his teammates."

Everything came together in 1981. Anderson completed 300 of 479 passes for 3,754 yards and 29 touchdowns. He completed 62.6 percent of his passes and had a passer rating of 98.4, good enough to be named the NFL's Most Valuable Player and Comeback Player of the Year.

The Bengals beat Buffalo and San Diego to advance to the Super Bowl, but they fell behind Joe Montana and the San Francisco 49ers 20–0 by halftime. The Bengals stormed back in the second half, but they still lost, 26–21, thanks in part to a huge goal-line stand by the 49ers in the third quarter.

"Every game, especially one you lose, there's always things you wish you had done," Gregg said of that Super Bowl. "But you can't do anything about it, so you don't worry about it. I was happy with these guys that we went to the Super Bowl. I wish we could have won. I think to this day that all these players would like to play that game over again, but that doesn't happen. It showed me what kind of character we had on that football team. We were going to be blown out, but we came back in that second half and came within six points of

DID YOU KNOW...

That Gregg won his sixth Super Bowl ring with the Dallas Cowboys in 1971?

them with a chance to do more. Those guys made up their minds the second half was going to be different, and it was."

Gregg led the Bengals to a 7–2 record in the strike-shortened 1982 season, and they lost to the New York Jets in the first round of the playoffs. The Bengals went 7–9 in 1983, and Gregg resigned after that season to take over the coaching job with the Packers. He felt it

TRIVIA

What's Forrest Gregg's full name?

Answers to the trivia questions are on pages 187–189.

was an opportunity he couldn't pass up, and he left on good terms with Paul Brown and his son Mike. In fact, Gregg now has a son living in Cincinnati and visits with Mike Brown whenever he gets back there.

"I did not have any problems working for Paul Brown," Gregg said, looking back at his time with the Bengals. "He had discipline throughout his organization. I was no stranger to that, having played for Vince Lombardi. Mike and I were talking one time. He said, 'I know my father is pretty tough at times.' I said, 'Hey, I've been chewed out by experts. This doesn't bother me at all.' I enjoyed working for him.

"One of the most enjoyable things I used to do…I knew all those old Browns players. I was always interested in knowing how he brought them together. As the season's going on, there's not too many opportunities to sit down and talk. We would always go to the visiting stadium on the day before a game for a warm-up workout, to get acclimated to the stadium and the field and what they looked like and what you could expect tomorrow. He liked doing that, and I liked doing that. So when we came back from the stadium to the hotel, a lot of times there would be a bus ride of 20 or 30 minutes or longer, and I would get him talking about how he put together that first team.… He brought a lot of those guys from Great Lakes Training Center. It was interesting to hear how that worked out and how he did that. That was something I really, really enjoyed. You could see that would inspire him to talk. He liked those guys and he said, 'I never knew whether they liked me or not.' But he didn't worry too much about it."

Gregg didn't worry about it either, but according to Lapham, he was well respected by his players.

"He was a good-hearted man," Lapham said. "He cared deeply about all the players. His philosophy was stern discipline, and strong discipline was the norm. That's what he was exposed to his whole career. He was a taskmaster, but he was fair. He wasn't two-faced about it. He wouldn't tell you one thing and tell the media another. You always knew where you stood with him. You could go into his office any time you wanted to and sit down and talk and he'd tell you the straight story."

A Most Colorful Coach

Steve Corn knows how lucky he is.

Corn is the athletics director at Pickens High School in Pickens, South Carolina, home of the Blue Flame. One of his neighbors volunteered to help out with the football team, a guy by the name of Sam Wyche.

Yes, that Sam Wyche.

The former head coach of the Cincinnati Bengals and the Tampa Bay Buccaneers owns a horse farm with his wife, a couple of miles from the school. In 2003, Wyche helped out with the team. When he went to the Buffalo Bills as quarterbacks coach for the 2004 and 2005 seasons, he kept in touch with the school. When he left the Bills, he returned to Pickens for the 2006 season. Corn was thrilled to have him back.

"He's a coaching genius," Corn said. "He has such a great offensive mind, but he makes it simple for the kids to understand. He's a great human being. Sure, there's an aura about him, but after a while, he's just like one of the guys. The kids don't really understand who they're dealing with. A couple of them rode a couple hours with him to one of our games. What I wouldn't give to ride in his truck for a couple hours. They don't get it like we do."

Most of the Pickens players probably weren't even born when Wyche took the Bengals to Super Bowl XXIII after the 1988 season. They probably don't know much of his football history. They know him as a coach. They know him as a magician. They know him as a substitute teacher. But not many of their teachers have as interesting a background as Wyche.

He was born January 5, 1945, in Atlanta. He attended North Fulton High School, where he was a backup quarterback. He dreamed of attending Georgia Tech, but the Yellowjackets didn't recruit him. He walked on as a freshman at Furman and eventually earned a scholarship from coach Bob King. More importantly, he met the woman who would become his wife, Jane Underwood.

Wyche was not drafted by the NFL, but after graduating in 1966, he started playing professional football for the Wheeling Ironmen in the minor-league Continental Football League. To help pay the bills, he also taught special education in Martins Ferry, Ohio. When he returned to the University of South Carolina to work on his master's degree, he became a graduate assistant to football coach Paul Dietzel and defensive backs coach Lou Holtz. Holtz had some connections, and he got Wyche a tryout with the expansion Cincinnati Bengals, who were to begin play in 1968 under legendary coach Paul Brown. The Bengals signed Wyche for $16,000, and sent him to work with quarterbacks coach Bill Walsh.

Yes, that Bill Walsh.

Wyche played backup quarterback for three seasons in Cincinnati, two in Washington (where he played in Super Bowl VII), one in Detroit, and one in St. Louis. He played in a total of 47 games

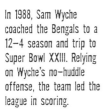

In 1988, Sam Wyche coached the Bengals to a 12–4 season and trip to Super Bowl XXIII. Relying on Wyche's no–huddle offense, the team led the league in scoring.

in his seven seasons, completing 116 of 222 passes for 12 touchdowns, with nine interceptions. Then he joined the coaching ranks, working for Walsh in San Francisco, where the 49ers would become a dynasty.

Wyche broke away to become the head coach at Indiana University in 1983, when the Hoosiers went 3–8. The next season he returned to the NFL, becoming the fifth coach in Bengals history. He replaced Forrest Gregg, who had taken the head coaching job with his old team, the Green Bay Packers.

Gregg had taken the Bengals to the Super Bowl after the 1981 season, but the team had tailed off to 7–9 in 1983. When Wyche came in, Ken Anderson was still the quarterback, but the Bengals had

Sam Wyche's Playing Statistics
Passing/Rushing

Year	Team	Games	Comp	Att	Pct.	Yards	Avg.	TD	INT	Att	Yards	TD
1968	Cincinnati	3	35	55	63.6	494	9.0	2	2	12	74	0
1969	Cincinnati	7	54	108	50.0	838	7.8	7	4	12	107	1
1970	Cincinnati	14	26	57	45.6	411	7.2	3	2	19	118	2
1971	Washington	1	0	0	0.0	0	0.0	0	0	1	4	0
1972	Washington	7	0	0	0.0	0	0.0	0	0	0	0	0
1974	Detroit	14	0	1	0.0	0	0.0	0	1	1	0	0
1976	St. Louis	1	1	1	100.0	5	5.0	0	0	0	0	0
Totals		47	116	222	52.3	1,748	7.9	12	9	45	303	3

drafted Boomer Esiason out of Maryland in the second round. In addition, they had sent running back Pete Johnson to San Diego for James Brooks.

Cincinnati started slowly that season, losing its first five games. But the Bengals won eight of the last 11 to finish one game short of Pittsburgh in the AFC Central. However, that group formed the foundation of the team that would return to the Super Bowl after the 1988 season.

No one expected that, not after the Bengals fell to 4–11 in 1987. But the 1988 season was magic. Relying on Wyche's no-huddle offense, the team finished 12–4 and led the league in scoring. Wyche and his players collected a ton of awards, including an NFL MVP award for Esiason. Linebacker Reggie Williams was named the *Sports Illustrated* Sportsman of the Year.

Unfortunately for the Bengals, they ran into an even more magical team in the Super Bowl—Walsh's San Francisco 49ers. Walsh was Wyche's mentor, and San Francisco quarterback Joe Montana had been Wyche's protege. In fact, Wyche had been on the 49ers' sideline when San Francisco beat Cincinnati in Super Bowl XVI after the 1981 season. But this time the pupil schooled the teacher. Montana threw a 10-yard touchdown pass to John Taylor with 34 seconds left, capping a 92-yard drive that lifted San Francisco to a 20–16 victory over Cincinnati in Super Bowl XXIII.

Wyche spent three more seasons in Cincinnati and four in Tampa Bay, but never again reached the heights of 1988.

Speaking his mind sometimes got the always-opinionated Wyche into trouble. Wyche, nicknamed "Wicky Wacky" in 1987 by a Steelers assistant coach, feuded with Houston coach Jerry Glanville, whom Wyche called a phony, and he ran up the score against the Oilers whenever he could. He alienated northeast Ohio when, while trying to get Cincinnati fans to stop throwing snowballs during a game against Seattle, he told the crowd over the public address system, "You don't live in Cleveland." (He later made amends by sitting in a dunk tank in Cleveland, raising $11,000 for the Salvation Army's Family Crisis Center.) And he was fined by the NFL when he refused to let a credentialed female reporter into his locker room after a *Monday Night Football* game in Seattle in 1990.

Sam Wyche's Coaching Record (Regular Season)

Year	Team	Record	Year	Team	Record
1984	Cincinnati	8–8	1991	Cincinnati	3–13
1985	Cincinnati	7–9	1992	Tampa Bay	5–11
1986	Cincinnati	10–6	1993	Tampa Bay	5–11
1987	Cincinnati	4–11	1994	Tampa Bay	6–10
1988	Cincinnati	12–4	1995	Tampa Bay	7–9
1989	Cincinnati	8–8			
1990	Cincinnati	9–7	Totals: 12 years, 84–107		

Still, after his coaching career, he became a popular motivational speaker and broadcaster, first at NBC and then at CBS. In 2000, he had a biopsy on lymph nodes in his chest. During the procedure, his left vocal cord was severed, leaving his voice a whisper. As a result, his speaking and broadcasting careers were curtailed. "That operation changed my life, my direction, my income, everything," he told the Associated Press.

In addition, he was diagnosed with cardiomyopathy, a disease of the heart muscle, which is currently being controlled with medication and a pacemaker. His health may have forced some changes in his life, but one thing that has not changed is his love of football. It is as strong as ever.

Wyche has not ruled out a return to the NFL, but for now, Pickens High School is the beneficiary of his decades of knowledge.

"We think he enjoys it," said Corn, the athletics director. "I know we enjoy him. I don't know what next year will bring for him. But he knows he's always welcome here."

A No-Nonsense Coach

The year 2006 was supposed to be the Cincinnati Bengals' year. The team was coming off a thrilling season in 2005, when it finished 11–5 and made the playoffs for the first time in 15 seasons. Heck, it was the first time since 1990 the team had finished over .500.

Coach Marvin Lewis was the man in Cincinnati. He'd never had a losing season. His three-year record of 27–21 gave him a winning percentage of .563, the best in the history of the franchise. And that includes Paul Brown, Forrest Gregg, and Sam Wyche.

Everywhere Lewis went, people wanted to shake his hand or pat him on the back. "Wait until next year," was a battle cry for the upcoming season, not an apology for the past season. The team's press guide even had the sites and dates of the next four Super

DID YOU KNOW...

That Marvin Lewis's boyhood sports idol was Roberto Clemente? But he told *The Sporting News* that his father, Marvin Lewis Sr., was the person he admired most because of his work ethic.

Bowls printed on the page adjacent to Lewis's biography. Just in case.

When Lewis was interviewed by *The Cincinnati Enquirer* before the opening of training camp in 2006, reporter Mark Curnutte asked if the 2006 team was the best he'd taken to training camp.

"Yes, by far," Lewis told Curnutte. "This is our best team from what we began with."

Of course, then he sounded a caution. "But it really doesn't matter how good your team is on paper," he told Curnutte. "It's how good you go play, prepare and play."

Indeed, a funny thing happened on the way to football immortality. A string of injuries and off-field incidents interrupted all the progress the team had made in Lewis's first three seasons. The coach who seemingly could do no wrong was being asked an entirely different set of questions.

Known as a players' coach as well as a disciplinarian, Lewis had to respond to inquiries about several players who were arrested in separate incidents. Others had substance-abuse issues—and that was in addition to the injuries. Before the Bengals played at Cleveland on November 26, there were 10 players on the injured list, plus another (Odell Thurman) suspended for violation of the league's substance-abuse policy. The injured list didn't even include three offensive linemen who had missed significant time—including right guard Bobbie Williams, who underwent an emergency appendectomy. At one time, the team was missing four linebackers from the top of its

Known as a players' coach as well as a disciplinarian, Marvin Lewis helped turn the losing Bengals around in 2005.

depth chart. (Ironically, quarterback Carson Palmer, whose left knee was severely injured in the playoff loss to Pittsburgh that ended the 2005 season, did not miss a game.)

When Cleveland reporters pressed Lewis about the injuries during the weekly conference call with media who cover the upcoming opponent, Lewis said, "We've talked enough about it. We've had injuries and moved on. Over the last three years we've drafted some good guys and they've had a chance to play football. In some ways that's good for you and good for your future. We just adjust and move on. That's all we can do."

Such a no-nonsense response and approach is no surprise to those who know Lewis. His attention to detail is so complete that he even started to prepare his football team for some adversity not long after Palmer's injury. In that conference call with the Cleveland media, Lewis was asked which was harder: trying to change the culture of a team that had been down for so long, as he'd had to do in 2003; or dealing with a team that wasn't living up to lofty expectations, which he faced in 2006.

"For coaches, the expectations don't change," said Lewis, whose team finished 8–8 in 2006, and 7–9 in 2007, missing the playoffs both years. "The biggest thing is the team being able to handle the adversity that you go through during a football season. It's going to be continuous. It's going to be all the time. You've just got to be able to handle it and adjust and work with it. We knew we were going to deal with adversity in a lot of different ways this year from the very start. Actually from the time we began as a team April 4, we began addressing those issues. Maybe they've helped us. It's hard to tell sometimes, but hopefully it has alleviated some of the stress that comes at a football team this way."

There's one other thing that helps Lewis get through tough times: he never loses his perspective. Lewis was born September 23, 1958, in McDonald, Pennsylvania, outside Pittsburgh. His father worked in the steel industry, swinging a sledgehammer in a facility that produced blast furnace coke. Lewis worked there one summer, too. He knows what it means to have a bad day at work. He knows having to answer questions about injuries—or anything else, for that matter—doesn't compare.

"It makes me appreciate how lucky we are to do what we do," Lewis said in that conference call. "I watched my dad go to the mill for 30 years until he couldn't go anymore. Having spent a summer there, I know what that's like. I know what those men have gone through. The nine weeks I spent in there were nine weeks of hell. So I'm appreciative of what I've had and the opportunities I've had, and that makes it real easy to come here every day and enjoy going to

Bengals Coaches

Coach	Record	Percentage
Paul Brown	55–59–1	.482
Bill Johnson	18–15–0	.545
Homer Rice	8–19–0	.296
Forrest Gregg	34–27–0	.557
Sam Wyche	64–68–0	.485
Dave Shula	19–52–0	.268
Bruce Coslet	21–39–0	.350
Dick LeBeau	12–33–0	.267
Marvin Lewis	42–39–0	.519

work…. I know my father didn't enjoy going to work. I'm fortunate that I can do that."

So instead of spending 30 years in the steel mill, Lewis has spent almost that long in coaching. His playing career took off at Fort Cherry High School, which also produced Marty Schottenheimer. Lewis was an all-conference quarterback and safety; he also earned letters in wrestling and baseball. He accepted a football scholarship to Idaho State, where he played linebacker as well as spending some time at quarterback and free safety. He was an All–Big Sky linebacker in 1978, 1979, and 1980.

While earning his bachelor's degree in physical education in 1981 and his master's in athletic administration in 1982, Lewis also started coaching the Idaho State linebackers. In his first year as an assistant coach in 1981, the Bengals went 12–1 and won the NCAA Division 1AA title. From Idaho State, Lewis took jobs as the linebackers coach at Long Beach State from 1985 to 1986, at New Mexico from 1987 to 1989, and at the University of Pittsburgh from 1990 to 1991.

After 11 seasons as a college coach and internships with the San Francisco 49ers and the Kansas City Chiefs, Lewis joined the NFL ranks in 1992 when Bill Cowher took over as the Steelers head coach. He stayed with Pittsburgh through the 1995 season and then joined the Baltimore Ravens as their defensive coordinator in 1996. In Baltimore, he fashioned a record-setting defense that was the envy of the league. In 2000, the Ravens set the NFL record for fewest points allowed in a 16-game season—165. The previous record had been 187. It was no coincidence that the Ravens won the Super Bowl that season.

Many thought such a performance would guarantee Lewis a position as head coach. He interviewed in Buffalo, Cleveland, Carolina, and Tampa before the Bengals broke with their tradition of promoting from within and reached out to hire Lewis from Washington, where he'd served as defensive coordinator and assistant head coach to Steve Spurrier in the 2002 season.

Much as he wanted to be a head coach in the NFL, though, Lewis accepted the Bengals' offer only after president and owner Mike Brown agreed to make substantial upgrades throughout the organization. Then Lewis set about getting everybody from the front-office executives to the locker-room attendants to buy into the resurrection of the franchise. Unlike several previous coaches, he also reached out to the community through hundreds of public appearances and the creation of the Marvin Lewis Community Fund, which has already donated more than $1 million to programs in the Cincinnati area.

Slowly, the creaky ship known as the Bengals started to turn around.

"To do what he did as fast as he did is almost incomprehensible; he raised the Titanic," ex-Bengal Solomon Wilcots told *The Sporting News*.

Though they started 1–4 in 2003 and 2004, they finished 8–8 in each of those seasons. To signal a total reversal of fortunes, they started 4–1 in 2005. After each of those seasons, Lewis was rewarded with a contract extension, the last of which would take him through the 2010 season. If he fulfills the entire eight years, Lewis will match the coaching longevity of Sam Wyche and Bengals founder Paul Brown, who currently share the team record for most seasons coached.

"Marvin has done a wonderful job for the football club on the field and off, and we want to reward his efforts and continue the relationship well into the future," Bengals president Mike Brown said, in a statement released by the team's media relations department on February 16, 2006, on the occasion of Lewis's third contract extension.

Before the 2004 season, Brown was asked how long he wanted Lewis to coach the Bengals. "My father [Paul Brown] coached in Cleveland for 17 years, and I felt that was too short," Brown said.

Chapter Four

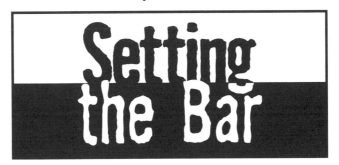

The Last Shall Be First

Bob Trumpy was one of the last college players drafted by the expansion Cincinnati Bengals in 1968, but he became one of their first stars.

It was not easy for Trumpy, a 6'6", 228-pound tight end from Utah who was taken in the 12th round, the 301st player taken overall. Nothing about playing for the legendary coach and founder of the team, Paul Brown, was easy.

"He made it very difficult," Trumpy said of Brown. "It took me a long time to understand [that] Cleveland ruined Paul Brown for us. Him being fired had a terrible, terrible effect on us. I don't think we knew that until we got a lot older and a lot smarter. We had fun as a group, but Paul never made it fun. There was nothing fun about football with Paul. Winning was fun. Knocking somebody down was fun. Scoring a touchdown, sure, that was fun. The first touchdown scored by the Cincinnati Bengals was by me, against Denver, on a pretty good play. My parents were in the stands. My wife was in the stands.

"I ran to the sideline and was jumping and hollering and screaming. Paul approached me, and I thought he was going to congratulate me. He said, 'Son, act like you've been there before.' I've heard a lot of people say that. But I'm telling you, he said that to me and it just deflated me terribly. [Tight-ends coach] Bill Walsh got me on the headset and said, 'That was a great catch, a great pattern. Don't let him bring you down. Congratulations.' My name was on the back of my jersey. I was playing in the NFL. I was going to get my $600 check on Tuesday. It was pretty nice. But he kind of blew that up. That's the way he ran the franchise."

Trumpy, born March 6, 1945, in Springfield, Illinois, lasted 10 years with the Bengals. He set several franchise records for tight ends that still stand and earned four trips to the AFL All-Star Game or the Pro Bowl, three of them in his first three seasons in the league. But when asked what it was like to play for Brown, Trumpy answered candidly.

"I didn't have a good first impression," he said. "I was 23, he was 60. I'm thinking, 'That's Paul Brown, the Hall of Famer? Are we sure we've got the right guy here?' The thing that stood out most was that he was incredibly organized. He used to pull out this faded manila envelope or folder. He'd kept track of the Browns as they moved from the All-America Football Conference to the NFL, and he used to compare us to them. I thought, 'Gee, that's interesting. But that's 30 years ago.' I had trouble understanding things like that. What difference does it make what they did 30 years ago? Collectively, we were 25 pounds heavier and two steps faster. But he was so organized he kept notes on the Browns' progress every day. I thought, 'That's meticulous.'

Bob Trumpy by the Numbers

4,600—career yards receiving
298—catches
128—games
15.4—average yards per catch
35—touchdowns
4—Pro Bowls

Bengals tight end Bob Trumpy was one of the last college players drafted by Cincinnati in 1968, but became one of the team's brightest stars.

"We practiced standing on the sidelines for the national anthem. We didn't do it once. We did it several times—how to stand there, where to stand, what to look like. At that time, coaches were kings in the NFL, and Paul was one of those guys who felt the team was a direct reflection of him and this was the way he wanted it to go. As things progressed, he kept our focus on doing our jobs and not worrying about winning or losing a game. We would end up winning games we shouldn't have.

"He was always very, very critical. He made a list of mistakes a player had made and reminded that player of the mistakes he made in front of everybody else. When we traveled, we used to see a movie the Saturday night before a football game. The business manager had three rules from Paul Brown about the movie: No R, no X, no Jim Brown. One time I think we saw *101 Dalmatians*.

"It was complete and utter organization down to the very last detail, which for a very young football team really helped. There were no roster limits then, and our first couple years we used to have 300 guys coming to training camp. They were always looking for somebody a little bit better. It never stopped.

"He did used to say things I thought were neat. For instance, when you'd go to get a newspaper out of one of those newspaper boxes, he'd say, 'Don't be a thief for a dime.' In other words, pay for each newspaper, don't just take a bunch of them out of the box. You wore the same thing at practice every day, the exact same thing. He was a stickler for being on time. Our second or third year, the first day of camp there was a tremendous thunderstorm about three minutes before we were to go out for our first practice. In three minutes it cleared up and we went out. I was standing about five feet from him and when it all cleared up, Paul turned around and said, 'He almost made a mistake.' I thought, 'Is he referring to God interrupting one of Paul Brown's practices?' Everybody started laughing. He started laughing, too, looking up at the sky. I thought, 'Geez, this is a powerful dude we're dealing with.'"

Trumpy paused for the laugh he knew was coming. As a longtime radio and television broadcaster who has informed and entertained fans for years, he knows how to tell a story and how to make the most of his deep voice. He's not used to telling stories about himself—at least not anymore. But he has a good tale to tell about getting ready for training camp in the summer of 1968.

"I was living in southern California when I was drafted, collecting bills for Beneficial Finance," he recalled. "I'd just gotten out of the Navy. On the day of the draft, my wife called me and told me I'd been drafted by the Bengals. Somebody in my wife's family had heard that. At that time, there wasn't ESPN. The commissioner's not on announcing the draft picks. I got a telegram. I walked in immediately and quit my job and looked around for a job that required a lot of physical strength, a job that would wear me out. I found a job at a company that made over-the-road travel trailers. It was called the Shasta Motor Coach Company or something like that. My brother-in-law worked there and got me the job. It was a very physical, demanding job, and that's what I wanted so I could get in shape.

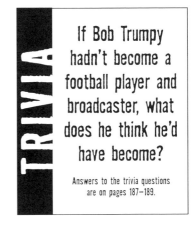

If Bob Trumpy hadn't become a football player and broadcaster, what does he think he'd have become?

Answers to the trivia questions are on pages 187–189.

"The second day I'm on the job, I'm driving home. I drive by what was then called Valley State Junior College. I noticed that there were some people out there practicing football. The next day after work I stopped and as I approached them, I noticed a green bag with a 'G' on it, which indicated Green Bay Packers to me. Lo and behold, the guy who was running the practice with 10 or 12 guys was Zeke Bratkowski, the backup quarterback to Bart Starr. It was a ragtag collection, no superstars other than Zeke Bratkowski.

"I introduced myself to Zeke and said, 'Do you need a receiver? I just got drafted by the Cincinnati Bengals, and I'm looking to work out. Here's my work schedule. How does that fit into your practice schedule?' Zeke told me when they met and where they met and asked if I could be there. I told him I couldn't, that I didn't get off work in time. He told me just to come out for the back half of the practice.

"The next day I go there and apparently there were no receivers for Zeke to throw to. After the second day we practiced together, he said, 'Look, I'm going to change the time of the practice to accommodate you, because you're the only receiver I've got.'

"That was in March. From that point forward, as I remember it, it was at least six days a week, maybe seven days a week. Over the

DID YOU KNOW...

That Bob Trumpy won the Illinois state title in the long jump as a senior at Springfield High School in 1963?

course of the next three months, we started each practice with about 75 or 100 up-downs, which Vince Lombardi loved. So when I went to camp, I knew for sure I was going to be in superb shape. Until then, I was just living on my athletic ability.

"The day before we broke up and went our separate ways, Zeke said to me, 'You're going to turn out to be a hell of a receiver. In Green Bay, we like big receivers. I don't know if you're going to make the Bengals, but I'm going to mention to our scouting staff that if the name Trumpy ever comes up on the waiver wire, the Green Bay Packers should look into acquiring him.'

"My head swelled to the size of the dome down at Epcot Center. I thought, 'Wow.' He'd never really said anything as we practiced. But I went to camp with Zeke Bratkowski's endorsement. That was big. So I went there knowing full well that whatever they wanted me to do, a professional quarterback thought I could do that. I carried that with me for quite a while. My mindset was, 'I can make this team.'

"When I went into the first meeting, there were 23 guys for three spots—two wide receivers and a tight end. I thought they might keep seven or eight people. The first official meeting was the night before camp started. The next day we weighed in. I thought if I could play two positions, wide receiver or tight end or both, I had a lot better chance to make the team. So the next morning when I weighed in, I carried a 10-pound weight underneath a towel. My actual weight was 208, and I weighed in at 218. I got away with that for one year, but the next five years I had to weigh in naked. They didn't trust me anymore. Two or three days after that, they began to work me out at some wide receiver but primarily tight end. So, I was never short on confidence."

In addition to the psychological lift he got from Bratkowski, Trumpy got a physical lift from tight-ends coach Bill Walsh, whom he credits for his success.

"We were the first team in the NFL to move the tight end," Trumpy said. "We didn't really know what the rules were. We had to call the league to find out what was allowed and what was not allowed. Back then, teams had strong safeties and weak [free] safeties, and the weak safeties never covered anybody. Bill Walsh came up with the idea to run patterns on the weak safety. We just blew our defense up doing that [in practice], so we incorporated it into our game plan. Frankly, Bill Walsh had to fight very hard to convince Paul Brown that it would work. Paul felt that it looked like we just didn't know where to line up. That bothered Paul Brown to no end. He wanted his team organized and giving the appearance that everybody knew exactly what they were going to do. I was the first tight end to split out wide, and I was the first tight end to go from one side to the other."

A Knack for the Ball

Cornerback Ken Riley had a goal every time he stepped onto the field for the Bengals. "I wanted to intercept everything that came my way," he said, with a laugh. There were days when opposing quarterbacks felt as if he did.

On December 12, 1976, in Joe Namath's last game as a New York Jet, Riley intercepted him twice—and backup Richard Todd once—in the Bengals' 42–3 victory, tying the Bengals' record for interceptions in a game.

On November 28, 1982, Riley intercepted Jim Plunkett three times in the Bengals' 31–17 victory over the Los Angeles Raiders.

Riley is the Bengals' career leader for interceptions, with 65 interceptions, 596 interception return yards, and five interception returns for touchdowns between 1969 and 1983. (His 15-season tenure with the team is second only to Ken Anderson's 16.) He led the Bengals (and the American Football Conference) with nine interceptions in 1976, a team record that stood for 30 years until Deltha O'Neal got 10 in 2005. Riley also had eight in 1983.

Riley, born August 6, 1947, in Bartow, Florida, used his skills as a former high school and college quarterback at Union Academy and Florida A&M, respectively—as well as some tricks he picked up in sandlot ball as a kid—to his advantage.

"Being a quarterback, I had a feel, a touch, for the ball," said Riley, who became a coach and athletics director at his college alma mater after his playing days. "Some of it was just God-given ability. I just had a knack. I'd see guys knocking balls down, and I'd think, 'Boy, they could be interceptions.'"

Riley, a gifted scholar and senior class president who was a candidate for a Rhodes Scholarship after college, was somewhat surprised when the Bengals selected him in the sixth round of the 1969 draft. He was not surprised they switched him to cornerback, however.

"I was really surprised to be drafted, being a quarterback and a black quarterback at that," he said. "At the college level, we didn't have many opportunities. But Paul Brown had a way of identifying talent. Back then, a lot of the black quarterbacks at predominantly black colleges were [versatile] athletes. I was not the first to be switched to defensive back; there were others as well. They drafted me as a defensive back/wide receiver. I was one of the original 'slashes.' When I got to camp, I was told I was going to play defensive back/cornerback. I was just happy to have the opportunity to show that I could play in the NFL…. A lot of guys were overlooked."

After that, he said he never gave the Rhodes Scholarship a second thought. "I didn't really pursue it," he said. "I think if I [had], I would

TRIVIA

Ken Riley is tied with Lemar Parrish, Tommy Casanova, Scott Perry, and Ray Griffin for most interception returns for a touchdown in a season, with two apiece. Who is the only one of those players to return two interceptions for touchdowns in one game?

Answers to the trivia questions are on pages 187–189.

have had a good opportunity. But once I make a decision, that's it. Once I started playing professional football all my energies were focused on doing that."

Instead, Riley became a student of the interception.

"I led the conference three times in interceptions—the last two times in 1982 and 1983," he said. "I got more interceptions in the latter part of my career, when they thought I had slowed down. When I got older, I got smarter. I used to bait them—show one thing and do something else. I had the quickness. I could accelerate. It was just a natural thing, something you can't explain."

Another thing that is hard to explain is why Riley, given his statistics, has never made the Pro Bowl or been seriously considered for the Pro Football Hall of Fame. As he points out, he had 25 more interceptions than Roger Wehrli, the former St. Louis Cardinals cornerback who was enshrined in the Pro Football Hall of Fame in 2007.

"There is no true method of selecting who's the best," said Riley, one of a number of former Bengals—including Ken Anderson, Tim Krumrie, Mike Reid, and Reggie Williams—who should be considered for the Hall of Fame. "In 1976, I led the conference with nine interceptions. Lemar Parrish, a teammate of mine who had been in the Pro Bowl before, made it, and he had been hurt half the year. People would say, 'How could that happen?'

Bengals Single-Season Interception-Return Yardage Leaders

Ray Griffin, 167 yards in 1979
Louis Breeden, 145 yards in 1981
Ken Riley, 141 yards in 1976

"Sportswriters and people who make those decisions don't really do what they're supposed to do. Just like the Hall of Fame. I have nothing against Roger Wehrli. But I've got 25 more interceptions than Roger Wehrli. Roger Wehrli never played in a Super Bowl. He played in a couple Pro Bowls. But the Pro Bowl is, a lot of times, [chosen by] name…. I don't think we pushed that like we should have. You can only go so far. I always thought your talent and actions would speak for you. I've never been a person who would go out and say, 'I'm the best.' Maybe that hurt me in a way, but that's just not my demeanor.

"When I was an athletics director, I was on the College Hall of Fame committee. I know how the process works, but it's not fair. A lot of times, you don't see these teams [because] they're in a small market. They're not nationally televised…. People don't know. It's very difficult.

"But if you have nine interceptions a year…no matter what market you're playing in, you're doing something right. You talk to the players. You ask them who were some of the better cornerbacks and they will tell you."

After his playing days, Riley was an assistant coach with the Green Bay Packers for two seasons and then became the head coach at Florida A&M. Between 1986 and 1993, the Rattlers compiled a 48–39–2 record, winning two Mid-Eastern Athletic Conference titles. Riley was named MEAC Coach of the Year twice. He served as the school's athletics director from 1994 to 2003. He retired for one year and then became a dean at Winter Haven High School, just outside his hometown of Bartow, Florida.

The Bengals' Best Quarterback?

Everybody has a favorite, and everybody has his or her own reasons why. But when Bengals founder Paul Brown wrote his autobiography in 1979, his opinion was clear. Granted, this was before Boomer Esiason came onto the scene, and before Carson Palmer was even born.

But Brown loved Ken Anderson.

"Ken Anderson ranks just behind Otto Graham as my best quarterback ever," Brown wrote in *PB: The Paul Brown Story*. "He has all of Otto's physical talents, as well as that one tremendously important attribute for any top-flight quarterback—stability. Stability is the basis for leadership, and leadership is a quality that transcends even a powerful arm or swift feet. A quarterback can never be a problem child, in my system.

"I don't take away the fact that fine quarterbacks like Bobby Layne and Sonny Jurgensen had their own lifestyles, but Graham and Anderson epitomize the kind of man I've always wanted to build with. I've rarely met a player with a better attitude toward people than Ken. He is purposeful, poised, well-rounded, and one of the pleasantest men I've ever known in any business. I've had a wonderful relationship with him ever since his first season with the Bengals."

Truth be told, Brown was at least a little concerned about drafting a quarterback who'd played at little Augustana College in Rock Island, Illinois. That's why he waited until the third round of the 1971 draft to take Anderson with the 67th pick. Anderson played sparingly behind Virgil Carter as a rookie, completing 72 of 131

Holding the team record for most completions in a game and highest completion percentage in a game, quarterback Ken Anderson was a cornerstone player for the Bengals in the early '80s.

passes for 777 yards and five touchdowns. But he became the starter in 1972—and held the job for the next 13 seasons.

"If there was any gamble in taking someone from such a small school, it was simply that he hadn't been exposed to the pressure of big-time competition," Brown said in his autobiography. "As it turned out, it never bothered him a bit because he had been born with poise, and from the start he looked like a veteran."

Anderson, born February 15, 1949, in Batavia, Illinois, virtually rewrote the Bengals' record book in his 16-year career. Schooled by Bengals assistant coach Bill Walsh in what is now called the West Coast offense, Anderson is still the Bengals' all-time leader in seasons, with 16; career passing attempts, with 4,475; career completions, with 2,654; career passing yards, with 32,838; career touchdown passes, with 197; and career interceptions, with 160. He was responsible for the longest pass in team history, 94 yards, to Billy Brooks on November 13, 1977, at Minnesota. He also gained 2,220 yards rushing—the team record for a quarterback—and scored 20 touchdowns on 397 carries. Anderson set single-season team records for average completions per game, with 24.2; average passing yards per game, with 277.2 yards; and completion percentage, with 70.55 percent, all in 1982. His single-season completion percentage is still an NFL record. He holds the team record for most completions in a game, with 40 on December 20, 1982, at San Diego; and highest completion percentage in a game, with 90.9 percent against Pittsburgh on November 10, 1974, when he hit 20 of 22 passes. He won four passing titles and was named to the Pro Bowl four times.

Anderson's former roommate, offensive lineman Dave Lapham, spent his career keeping Anderson safe. But Lapham said Anderson was always upright.

"A great guy, a family guy…very solid in every way," Lapham recalled. "A guy who was totally accountable, totally prepared for every game. Forget about bending a rule, he never even thought about stretching a rule. A total team guy.

"The thing about Kenny is that [whether] we were 12–4 and he was the MVP of the league, or we were 4–12 and he was getting sacked and beaten up, he was the same guy. Very consistent. Very dependable. He wasn't affected by anything, very even-keeled. I think

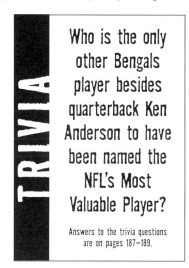

TRIVIA

Who is the only other Bengals player besides quarterback Ken Anderson to have been named the NFL's Most Valuable Player?

Answers to the trivia questions are on pages 187–189.

that was one of the reasons he performed so well for so long. He didn't get real high with the highs or real low with the lows."

Anderson's best season overall was 1981, when he completed 300 of 479 passes for 3,754 yards and 29 touchdowns. He completed 62.6 percent of his passes and had a passer rating of 98.4, good enough to be named the NFL's Most Valuable Player and the Comeback Player of the Year. He also rushed for 320 yards and one touchdown. He led the Bengals to their first playoff victory, 28–21, over Buffalo, and their first AFC title, with a 27–7 victory over San Diego.

In Super Bowl XVI, Anderson completed 25 of 34 passes for 300 yards and two touchdowns, with two interceptions. He also rushed for 15 yards and one touchdown. (At the time, his 25 completions and his completion percentage of 73.5 were both Super Bowl records.) But the Bengals lost, 26–21.

Cris Collinsworth was a receiver on that team. He caught 67 passes for 1,009 yards that season, most of them from Anderson.

"Kenny Anderson was a student of the game, the serious businessman in the huddle, the most accurate passer of all time," Collinsworth said. "If he threw it down at your knees, that meant catch it and duck, because somebody's about to kill you. If he led it out in front of you, you knew nobody was there and you could run

By the Numbers

Longest Passes in Bengals History

- 94 yards: Ken Anderson to Billy Brooks, November 13, 1977, at Minnesota (touchdown)
- 90 yards: Virgil Carter to Speedy Thomas, September 19, 1971, versus Philadelphia (touchdown)
- 88 yards: Jeff Blake to Darnay Scott, September 17, 1995, at Seattle (touchdown)
- 86 yards: Boomer Esiason to Eddie Brown, November 6, 1988, versus Pittsburgh (touchdown)
- 85 yards: Ken Anderson to Isaac Curtis, December 12, 1976, at New York Jets (touchdown)

as hard as you could. He was a little bit more on the conservative side. He didn't want to take chances and wanted to make sure he wasn't going to be intercepted."

Anderson had another great season in 1982, but the Bengals couldn't get past the New York Jets in the first round of the playoffs, losing 44–17. He remained the starter in 1983 and 1984, but was replaced as the starter by Boomer Esiason in the third game of the 1985 season. He retired after the 1986 season.

After working in broadcasting in Cincinnati for several years, Anderson became the Bengals quarterbacks coach from 1993 to 1996 and 2001 to 2002, and served as the team's offensive coordinator from 1996 to 2000 under Bruce Coslet. In 2003, he became the quarterbacks coach for the Jacksonville Jaguars, coached their wide receivers for one season, and then shifted back to quarterbacks coach, working with Byron Leftwich.

"Kenny, first of all, is a good person," Jacksonville coach Jack Del Rio told the *Dayton Daily News*. "He's a good coach. He's got a wealth of experience on offense. He obviously had a great career…as a player and then as a coach. We're happy to have him. He's done a very, very good job with Byron, developing a young quarterback, and we're just pleased with all the work he's done."

Bengals quarterback Carson Palmer remembers meeting Anderson at the NFL Combine in 2003, shortly after Anderson joined the Jacksonville staff.

"He got real emotional," Palmer told the *Daily News*. "He's a very passionate person and you could tell that Cincinnati had a very big place in his heart, that the city meant something special to him. He loved the people, loved the fans, a good guy for me to run into. He had just been let go, and for a guy to be that emotional about a place, and have that much love for an organization, definitely spoke a lot to me. He spent so much time here and had so many good years here. He just had a really good run."

Anderson said he just wanted to reassure Palmer.

"People were concerned about him coming to a franchise that hadn't had success in a while," Anderson told the *Daily News*. "I just told him that Cincinnati was a great city to live and play in, and that it was also a great organization to be a part of. It has a great owner [Mike Brown] who wants to win. Obviously, Cincinnati and the Bengals organization mean quite a lot to me. I spent 30-plus years of my life in the city and connected with the organization. To be part of a young franchise and see it grow and become successful made me very proud."

When Jacksonville failed to make the playoffs after the 2006 season, Anderson was let go as part of a number of changes Del Rio made to his staff. In 2007, Anderson moved on to the Pittsburgh Steelers as their quarterbacks coach, working with Ben Roethlisberger.

A Man for All Seasons

Dave Lapham has seen it all in Cincinnati.

Since joining the Bengals as a third-round draft choice out of Syracuse in 1974, he has spent only two seasons away from the team—in 1984 and 1985, when he played with the New Jersey Generals of the United States Football League.

He played for Paul Brown, the founder of the franchise. He went to Super Bowl XVI with coach Forrest Gregg after the 1981 season. Then he covered Super Bowl XXIII after the 1988 season as a broadcaster. The 2007 season marked his 22nd season in that role.

The only thing Lapham really missed was the Bengals' start-up.

"The first couple of training camps were wild," he said. "I didn't witness that, but I've heard stories."

After playing with the Bengals for 10 years and then watching them for twice as long, Lapham is in a unique position to offer some historical perspective. He was asked if the 2006 edition of the Bengals reminded him of any other Bengals team.

"I think every team is its own animal, but there are some similarities offensively between this football team and both teams that went to the Super Bowl," Lapham said in 2006. "They both had league-MVP quarterbacks—Kenny Anderson and Boomer Esiason—and Carson Palmer is cut from that cloth. He's dynamic at the quarterback position. He's got a stable of receivers—Chad Johnson, T.J. Houshmandzadeh. The 1981 team had Isaac Curtis and Cris Collinsworth. The 1988 team had Eddie Brown and Tim McGee, and Cris Collinsworth was still there. Those teams had a great running back. In 1981 it was Pete Johnson. In 1988, it was Ickey Woods and James Brooks. This year's [2005] running back is Rudi Johnson. So they all had a lot of weapons offensively, and very solid offensive lines that gave the skill players an opportunity to perform their magic. I see a lot of similarities with this offense. The only thing those offenses had that this offense doesn't is a pass-receiving tight end. We had Danny Ross in 1981. In 1988, it was Rodney Holman. They were both Pro Bowl tight ends. That's not part of the offensive attack in this year's team as opposed to those two Super Bowl years."

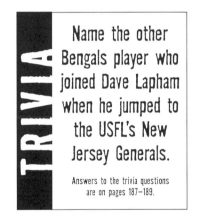

TRIVIA: Name the other Bengals player who joined Dave Lapham when he jumped to the USFL's New Jersey Generals.

Answers to the trivia questions are on pages 187–189.

Defensively, though, Lapham sees some differences.

"It depends on which defense you're talking about," he said. "This year's [2005] defense is very inconsistent. They gave up 42 points in a half to the San Diego Chargers. That was a club record, second-most in NFL history. They looked very, very poor doing it. But then they gave up only 23 points total in their next three games.

"They don't have any real big, big names, defensive-player-of-the-year types. But they're playing well as a group. They're understanding where they're supposed to be, what they're supposed to do, and they're starting to play faster because they are understanding those things. The 1988 defense was about the middle of the pack, like this one. The 1981 defense was pretty good. By 1983 they were number one in the NFL defensively. I'd say this defense is probably more similar to the 1988 defense."

Of course, between 1988 and 2006 there were some lean years in Cincinnati. Fans would show up to the Jungle in Riverfront Stadium, and later Cinergy Field and Paul Brown Stadium, wearing bags over their heads. As a former player, it was hard for Lapham to watch as a broadcaster.

"There was a 15-year stretch where they were never better than .500," he said. "The support was dwindling, but there was a core group of season-ticket holders of 35,000 or whatever, that come hell or high water was supporting the Cincinnati Bengals.… It is a good football town. They still drew some nice crowds to a new stadium when they were 2–14. The product just wasn't that good.

"The NFL is built for parity, and 50 percent of the games are decided by a touchdown or less and 33 percent by a field goal or less, so usually they're competitive. So it wasn't just that the Bengals were losing, it was how they were losing. They were getting crushed. They were losing by double-digit scores or three touchdowns. In the NFL that's just unheard-of. People were like, 'Oh geez, here we go again.'

"As a former player, as an alum, you want your high school to do well…you want your college to do well…and you want your pro team to do well. I'd go around the country and guys would say, 'What the hell is wrong with the Bengals? For all these years, they've had all these high draft choices.' I'd say, 'I wish I could answer you, but it's a multitude of things.'

"Eventually they reinvented themselves, though, and here they are. That's the amazing thing. The fans are getting rewarded now with the success of the franchise under Marvin Lewis. Their support has been steadfast. But they've definitely embraced the organization under Marvin."

According to Lapham, the hiring of Lewis signaled a change in how the Bengals operated.

"The biggest difference with this version of the Cincinnati Bengals is that for the first time, they reached outside of the actual organization in terms of a former player or former assistant coach [not being hired as] the head coach," he said. "They had always gone in that direction. It was either one of Paul Brown's assistants who he had total faith in, or one of Paul Brown's assistants that Mike Brown had total faith in, or a former player like Bruce Coslet. They had never reached outside the family, so to speak. Now with Marvin Lewis, they broadened their horizons and brought in a guy who witnessed the Pittsburgh Steelers going to the Super Bowl and what they did to get there, and the Baltimore Ravens. I think the difference is that there's a lot more openness to newer ideas, with Marvin Lewis's exposure outside the organization."

Because he was an outsider, Lewis worked hard to gain acceptance.

"I've never seen a coach anywhere be as visible and accessible as he has been to the community from day one," Lapham said. "He established the Marvin Lewis Community Fund, which has raised millions of dollars for various needs in the community, as well as for multiple sclerosis. He has a brother-in-law who suffers from MS. They've made significant contributions to that as well.

DID YOU KNOW...

That there's a famous comic book writer also named David Lapham? He is best known for the independent comic book *Stray Bullets*.

"He wants his players to give back to the community and be involved in the community, and he does it by example. I don't think there's another head coach in the league who is more involved directly in the community in terms of giving back and being high-profile and visible than Marvin is here in Cincinnati. Before he drafted Carson Palmer and people like that, he was the face of the franchise. His first draft pick was the number one pick in the entire draft, and he wanted Carson Palmer to become a face of the organization. He's done a great job adding additional faces, but Marvin first and foremost was the new face of the organization."

Lapham remains one of the most familiar faces, though.

Born June 24, 1952, in Melrose, Massachusetts, he came to the Bengals from Syracuse, where he lettered in three seasons and was a team captain. The Bengals made him a third-round draft choice, and he wound up playing all five positions on the offensive line, protecting quarterback Ken Anderson, who just happened to be his roommate. After those two seasons in the USFL, Lapham became the color analyst for the Bengals' radio broadcasts. He also works as a reporter and analyst for Cincinnati's WLWT-TV, NBC Channel 5. He also works on Fox Sports Net's broadcasts of Big-12 conference games. In previous years, he broadcast NFL games for NBC and Fox and worked on the NFL Europe League's World Bowl Game for Sporting News Radio.

The Legend Stays Close to Home

Archie Griffin is a legend in Ohio.

The only two-time Heisman Trophy winner in history, the former Ohio State star is revered for his skill on the football field and respected for his accomplishments off it. In this football-mad state, there are only three men who could challenge Griffin in a popularity contest—Jim Brown, Woody Hayes, and Paul Brown—and Griffin is associated with all three of them.

As a kid growing up in Columbus, Griffin idolized Jim Brown, the star running back of the Cleveland Browns, and patterned his game after Brown's. As a hotshot high school star from Columbus Eastmoor High School, Griffin chose to stay at home and play for Hayes and the Buckeyes, a decision that paid dividends for all involved.

Then Paul Brown made Griffin the Bengals' number one draft choice, which allowed him to continue his football career about 100 miles from home.

Paul Brown retired from coaching after the 1975 season, so Griffin never got to play for the venerable coach who founded the Browns and the Bengals. He never developed the same sort of close relationship with Brown that he had with Hayes. But Griffin was with the Bengals from 1976 to 1983, and Brown ran the operation that whole time.

TRIVIA

Which Bengals player wore No. 45 before Archie Griffin?

Answers to the trivia questions are on pages 187–189.

Griffin definitely saw some similarities between Brown and Hayes.

"They both were pretty doggone tough," said Griffin, now the president of the Ohio State University Alumni Association. "The leadership aspect was evident on both their parts. Paul Brown certainly was a great leader. You could just tell in his actions and [by] how he carried himself. You knew he wanted the Bengals to be successful. I felt that, any time I had any contact with him."

Although he had admired Jim Brown, Griffin really had not envisioned a career in pro football.

"When I came to college, it wasn't a goal of mine to play pro football," said Griffin, whose father worked three jobs to support his eight children, including seven sons. "I wanted to use the game to get a college education. Once I got to college, I thought, 'You might be

Running back Archie Griffin, the only back-to-back winner of the Heisman Trophy, received the honor in 1974 and 1975 at Ohio State.

able to play pro football.' It wasn't a big goal, but I thought it would give me a quick start to the rest of my life. After my junior year, I knew I'd probably get that shot. Then I started looking at a future in pro football. But what was most important at that time was finishing the goal I started and getting an education."

After graduating a quarter early with a degree in industrial relations, Griffin went to work for the Bengals. In 1976, the team went 10–4, and Griffin had 625 yards rushing and 138 receiving. In 1977, they were 8–6, and Griffin had 549 yards rushing and 240 receiving. But the Bengals went 4–12 in 1978, a tough adjustment for a player who lost a total of five games in college.

Although Griffin had his best season as a pro in 1979, with 688 yards rushing and 417 receiving, the Bengals went 4–12 again. And they were 6–10 in 1980, when Griffin had just 260 yards rushing and 196 receiving.

"When you have the kind of record we had, it's not fun," Griffin admitted. "1978, 1979, and 1980 were tough years. We just could not put it all together. No question, it is work. You go in at 8:00 AM and leave at five or six in the evening. It certainly is a job. If you don't love the game, it's hard to do."

Of course, Griffin loved the game, so he persevered, as did all the Bengals. They were rewarded in 1981, when they finished with a 12–4 record and advanced to the Super Bowl before losing to San Francisco, 26–21.

Griffin's role was reduced that season. He had just 47 carries for 163 yards and 20 catches for 160 yards. In the Super Bowl, he had one carry, picking up four yards. The next season, he had just 12 carries for 39 yards and 22 catches for 172 yards, and he missed the 1983 season with a torn stomach muscle. For his career, he had 691 carries for 2,808 yards, averaging 4.1 yards per carry. He also had 192 catches for 1,607 yards, an 8.4-yard average. He ran for seven touchdowns and caught six touchdown passes.

Some might be disappointed with those statistics, or with the length of a career cut short by injury. But not Griffin.

"I wasn't disappointed at all," he said. "When I started, I thought I would play only five years. But I played eight years. Cincinnati was a pass-oriented ball club, so I was not going to get the carries I got in college. I probably carried less than 10 times a game. With those carries, you're not going to get 1,000 yards a year. You need at least 200 or 250 carries to get 1,000 yards. So I switched my goal; I wanted to average five yards a carry. I didn't quite make it. But averaging five yards a carry is a tough thing to do. If you average four yards a carry, you're doing very, very well.

"In Cincinnati, I think I proved to people I wasn't just going to be a running back. I could do things other than carry the ball. I could catch the ball out of the backfield, too. At Ohio State, we didn't pass very much. I was proud people could see I could do things with the ball after catching a pass. They weren't used to seeing me do that. I was able to exhibit skills that I thought I always had but didn't get a chance to use."

All those skills were on display at Eastmoor, which now plays on Archie Griffin Field. After alternating at fullback in a wing-T offense as a sophomore, Griffin became the featured back, rushing for more than 1,000 yards as a junior and 1,737 yards as a senior, when he had 29 touchdowns and 170 points to lead Eastmoor to its second

Fab Four

Archie Griffin is a member of the following:
- The Ohio State University Athletics Hall of Fame
- The National Football Foundation Hall of Fame
- The Rose Bowl Hall of Fame
- The National High School Hall of Fame

DID YOU KNOW...

That Archie Griffin is the only player to have started in four Rose Bowls?

straight city title. He also played linebacker as a sophomore and junior, wrestled, competed in the shot put, and ran relays in track while maintaining a B average and graduating in the top 25 percent of his class. As a senior, he was named Ohio's co–Back of the Year and a Sunkist All-American.

At 5'9" and 180 pounds, Griffin was small but mighty. He got off on the wrong foot at Ohio State when he fumbled his first carry as a freshman, in the fourth quarter of the season opener at Iowa. The next week against North Carolina, he entered the game in the first quarter with the Buckeyes trailing, 7–0. He wound up running for a school-record 239 yards as the Buckeyes rallied for a 29–14 victory. He started every game after that, rushing for an Ohio State-record 5,589 yards and 26 touchdowns. He led the Buckeyes to four straight Big Ten championships and four straight Rose Bowls.

Griffin became the first OSU sophomore to rush for 1,000 yards (he ended up with 1,577). He was a first-team UPI All-America selection, and he won the *Chicago Tribune*'s Silver Football as the Big Ten Player of the Year. As a junior in 1974, he rushed for a then-school record 1,695 yards, and won the Heisman Trophy and a second Silver Football. He was an All-America selection and was named the UPI and Walter Camp Player of the Year. He won all but the Silver Football as a senior, when he rushed for 1,450 yards. *The Sporting News* named him Man of the Year in 1975. Between his sophomore and senior seasons, Griffin ran for 100 or more yards in a NCAA-record 31 consecutive regular-season games.

In his career, he rushed for more than 100 yards in 33 games, also an NCAA record; his average of 6.13 yards per carry is yet another

NCAA record. Not counting bowl games, Griffin rushed for 5,177 yards on 845 carries. The 5,177 yards ranks fifth in NCAA history. After his senior year, Griffin received the NCAA's prestigious Top Five Award for combined excellence in athletics, academics, and leadership. It is the highest award the NCAA can bestow.

Small wonder No. 45 became the first Ohio State player to have his number retired. He was so honored on September 30, 1999.

Chapter Five

Getting His Kicks in Cincinnati

Of all the things he has accomplished in his football career—and there are many—the thing place-kicker Jim Breech is most proud of is his perfect record in overtime.

In 14 seasons in the National Football League—13 of them with the Bengals—Breech made all nine of his overtime field-goal attempts, an NFL record he shares with Buffalo's Steve Christie.

"When you make big kicks, important kicks, it's the only way you can help your team," Breech said. "For 58 minutes, I'm a fan or a spectator. A game-winning kick is the best way to be a good teammate."

From 1980 to 1992, Breech was a great teammate. He is the Bengals' all-time leading scorer, with 1,151 points on 225 field goals and 476 extra points; his totals in those categories are Bengals career records as well. He is tied with Anthony Muñoz, Joe Walter, and Rich Braham for fourth place on the list of most seasons with the team, and his 120 points in 1985 and 115 in 1981 rank fourth and fifth on the team's list of single-season scoring.

His single most productive day came on October 29, 1989, when he kicked eight extra points—a team single-game record—in a 56–23 victory over Tampa Bay. He is second in NFL history on the list of all-time scoring in consecutive games, with 186 consecutive games.

Jim Breech is the Bengals' all–time leading scorer; who is second on that list?

Answers to the trivia questions are on pages 187–189.

Counting his 18 field goals and 41 extra points with Oakland in 1979, Breech made 243 of 340 field goals (71.5 percent), 517 of 539 extra points (95.9 percent), and scored 1,246 total points in 14 seasons in the NFL.

There's a certain irony in all this, given how Breech actually wound up in Cincinnati. Born April 11, 1956, in Sacramento, California, Breech was a quarterback and kicker at Sacramento High School, where he also played basketball and baseball. He was a great admirer of kicking legend Jan Stenerud, and he started wearing the No. 3 in honor of the soccer-style kicker.

After graduating from the University of California in 1978, Breech was selected in the eighth round of the NFL draft by the Detroit Lions, but didn't make the team. He spent the 1979 season with the Los Angeles Raiders. But during the 1980 preseason, the Bengals cut Chris Bahr, and the Raiders cut Breech to make room for Bahr.

"While [coach] Tom Flores was cutting me, Chris Bahr was driving back and forth outside so we didn't end up there together," Breech recalled. "Steve Ortmeyer, who was our special teams coach and is now the special teams coach at Kentucky, told me it was the most unfair decision he'd ever seen in professional sports."

Breech got a job at a paper company in Emeryville, California, and waited for another football team to call. It took 10 weeks, but the first team to call was the Cleveland Browns. Assistant player-personnel director Paul Warfield told Breech that Browns kicker Don Cockroft had a sore back and the Browns were looking for some insurance. Breech thought he was all set, but the Browns never called back.

The Bengals did, though, and they proved to be a perfect match. Years later when Breech saw Warfield and recounted this story, Warfield laughed and said, "I should have called you back."

It was lucky for Cincinnati—and Breech—that he didn't. In addition to being a dependable field-goal kicker and almost automatic on extra points during the regular season, Breech was a key cog on the Bengals' two Super Bowl teams, never missing a field goal or extra point in either Super Bowl. In Super Bowl XVI, he kicked three extra points, but the Bengals' rally came up short in a 26–21 loss to the San Francisco 49ers. In Super Bowl XXIII, he kicked field goals of 34 and 43 yards, and then he made an extra point. When he kicked his third field goal of the day, a 40-yarder that gave the Bengals a 16–13 lead with 3:20 left, it looked as if he might become the first kicker named Most Valuable Player in the Super Bowl. But, as any Bengals fan knows, that was not to be. Joe Montana rallied the 49ers to a 20–16 victory, and Jerry Rice ended up as the MVP.

By the Numbers

Jim Breech: Points per Season with the Bengals

Season	Points	Season	Points	Season	Points
1980	23	1985	120	1990	92
1981	115	1986	101	1991	96
1982	67	1987	97	1992	88
1983	87	1988	89		
1984	103	1989	73	Total	1,151

Breech doesn't dwell on that, but he admitted that in the weeks leading up to the Super Bowl every year, when Super Bowl XXIII is often rebroadcast, it's hard not to look back and wonder "What if?"

He says, "I occasionally watch and think back to what was going on and think, 'If we would have just done this.…' But for the most part, I just watch and root for the kickers to do well."

He said kickers have evolved tremendously since the days he played. "There are more technical things, more video. There are camps. Everybody starts earlier. So many kids play soccer and come into it that way. They're better athletes. It can be lucrative if you do it well."

For all those reasons, Breech figures that his scoring record for the Bengals will eventually fall, even though few players remain with one team as long as he did.

Breech still lives in the Cincinnati area, where he is a sales executive for the Hauser Group, an insurance firm. He and kickers Doug Pelfrey and Shayne Graham are very involved in an organization called Kicks for Kids, which provides help and support for children with environmental challenges. "We give them hope," Breech said.

He did that for Cincinnati fans for years.

Chatting up a Storm

Cris Collinsworth had no idea he could make a living talking.

"You want to talk about a good life," the former Bengals Pro Bowl wide receiver said, still sounding somewhat incredulous. "If you go from playing football to talking about football the rest of your life, that's a pretty good life."

The always chatty and insightful Collinsworth seemed like a natural to become the first color analyst for the NFL Network, teaming with play-by-play man Bryant Gumbel as the network expanded its repertoire to include live game coverage during the 2006 season. Of course, fitting the Thursday and Saturday night games into Collinsworth's schedule was no easy feat. He was already acting as a studio analyst and cohost of NBC's *Football Night in America* on Sundays and working on HBO's *Inside the NFL* on Wednesdays.

That's a lot of talking—even for Collinsworth. But he said he couldn't pass up the chance to work with Gumbel.

"Basically, I begged him to do it," Collinsworth said. "I told him, 'Listen, if you're not interested in doing this, I'm not doing it either.'

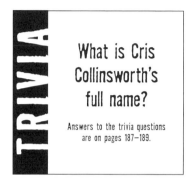

TRIVIA

What is Cris Collinsworth's full name?

Answers to the trivia questions are on pages 187–189.

I just look at it as a great opportunity to work with a guy who has a bigger view of the world and a grander view of the world than what happened on third-and-10 last week in Kansas City. That's what makes it exciting.

"I know that the chemistry, the play-by-play skills, all that stuff's going to happen. But I'm not interested in doing this unless I can engage in a conversation with a guy who's smarter than I am. And he is.

"I really have tremendous respect for Bryant Gumbel. How many partners are you going to have who have interviewed every president of the United States for the past 20 or 25 years, world leaders on a variety of topics around the world, who have covered the collapse of the Cold War and cold beer at the same time? He's just one of the smartest guys I've ever been around. Every once in a while, has he messed up whether it's first-and-10 or second-and-nine? He has. I have, too. But my point is, who cares? Here's a guy with a perspective that some slick 25-year-old play-by-play guy is never going to have."

Collinsworth wasn't much more than 25 when he made his broadcasting debut. A second-round draft choice from the University of Florida in 1981, he played eight productive seasons with the Bengals, earning three Pro Bowl nods and two trips to the Super Bowl. The 6'4", 190-pound string bean caught 417 passes for 6,698 yards and had 36 touchdowns in 107 games.

He probably did at least one interview for every one of those yards, too.

When *Sports Illustrated* wrote a cover story about him during his rookie season, the piece by John Underwood seemed like one long quote. There are 15 straight paragraphs of quotes near the beginning of the story. In the 56 paragraphs that follow, 24 are quotes— although truthfully, not all of them are by Collinsworth. Some of them are quotes about him.

That cover story, on December 14, 1981, was a turning point in Collinsworth's career. It came after he scored two touchdowns in a 41–21 victory at Cleveland on November 29, 1981, the season the Bengals made their first Super Bowl appearance. Collinsworth knew he'd made it after being featured on the cover of the premier sports magazine in the world. He was finally convinced he was going to have a career in pro football.

"I was so used to being broke," he said. "I was a typical college student. I had some money, but my parents bought me a Mercury Bobcat. If you couldn't afford a Pinto, you bought a Bobcat. When I came to Cincinnati, I had a place to live. But I really only had the basics—a bed, a couch, a TV. I would only allow myself to buy something for myself or the apartment if I played a good game. That was my motivation. Eventually I got a stereo, and I slowly sort of filled the condo. But the one thing I wouldn't do—it was a superstition—I would never get a new car. They would all make fun of my car. Finally, when I got on the cover of *Sports Illustrated*, I decided it was time. I bought a baby-blue Porsche."

Collinsworth lasted through the transition from Forrest Gregg to Sam Wyche, as well as the passing of the torch from quarterback Ken

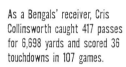
As a Bengals' receiver, Cris Collinsworth caught 417 passes for 6,698 yards and scored 36 touchdowns in 107 games.

Anderson to quarterback Boomer Esiason. He'd been planning for the end of his career long before it came, after the 1988 season.

"I actually was in law school [at the University of Cincinnati] during my final two or three years playing, taking classes at night and [in] the morning," said Collinsworth, who had an accounting degree from the University of Florida. "It took me five years to get through it, but I eventually did get my degree. So when I got cut by the Bengals, I was just going to finish law school and become an attorney. Then I started getting calls. I got a call from HBO two days after I was cut. Probably a week later I got a call from NBC asking if I would do games. Then a local radio station called. It just kind of fell into place. I wasn't really sure how it happened or why it happened. I tell people the one thing I learned after five years of law school is that I didn't want to be a lawyer. This is a little bit better career path for me."

Born on January 27, 1959, at Miami Valley Hospital in Dayton, Collinsworth's family moved to Titusville, Florida, when he was four years old. He was a quarterback at Astronaut High School, where he also won a state title in the 100-yard dash. When he got to Florida, coach Doug Dickey switched him to wide receiver, paving the way for those three Pro Bowl appearances.

Of course, Collinsworth has also won six Emmys for his television work. He was asked if he was more proud of the Pro Bowls or the Emmys.

"I hate to say it," he answered. "From the moment we were children and the first time we played ball in the backyard, we all wanted to be the best athlete. The first time I was told in my rookie year that I was going to the Pro Bowl, I thought I was going to pass out. I never even considered the possibility that was going to happen. At least they nominate you, so you have some idea on the Emmys. They're pretty close. I have to tell you the truth, I kind of scoff at television a little bit. Now wait a minute—they're going to pay me more than I ever made playing football for talking? This is crazy.

"Every once in a while when I go to a party and somebody doesn't know who I am and they ask what I do for a living and I say, 'I watch football games,' they'll start laughing and say, 'No, really, what do you do for a living?' And I say, 'I watch football games.' Then I've got to talk about them for the next hour and a half."

Not that that's a problem.

DID YOU KNOW...

That Collinsworth's father's name was Abraham Lincoln Collinsworth and that he played on the NCAA championship basketball team at Kentucky in 1958?

The Best Ever?

From day one, Forrest Gregg knew Anthony Muñoz was going to be an incredible player. Shortly after Gregg was hired to coach the Bengals in 1980, the team was preparing for the draft. Gregg still remembers senior vice president of player personnel Pete Brown, son of the Bengals' legendary founder and first coach Paul Brown, saying, "If I had a vote right now, I'd vote that we draft Anthony Muñoz."

Paul Brown, who was still the team's general manager at the time, told Gregg he should go out to the University of Southern California and take a look at Muñoz, who'd had three knee injuries in his four seasons of collegiate football.

Gregg got to the Los Angeles campus at 9:00 AM and watched four hours of film on Muñoz. That afternoon, he met with Muñoz and worked him out.

"I had drawn some conclusions watching the film," Gregg recalled. "The thing I questioned was his knee. I looked at it. The two things I remember most: he had shorts on and had the biggest legs I'd ever seen. He also had more hair than any ballplayer I'd ever had anything to do with.

"I took him out and ran him through some drills. It was obvious this guy had great athletic skills. He was big as a house. He probably weighed 275 or 285. I didn't ask. I saw what his mobility factor was. It was easy to see this guy had talent.

"I decided to watch him move against an opponent, [but] the only opponent he had out there was me. So I thought I would go through some things and he'd react. I thought, 'Okay, I'll give you a few pass rushes.' I figured I was going to set him up. I made an outside rush, he shadowed me and pushed me with his hands. Then I made an inside rush and he reacted to that with ease.

"Then I thought I had him set up, so I came off the ball like I was going inside but I went outside. When I went outside, he jammed me and knocked me flat on my rear. He had a strange look on his face and apologized as he picked me up off the ground. I said, 'Oh no, I asked for that.'

"Then I went back and watched some more film. I think he had come back at the end of the year and played in the Rose Bowl. So I was able to see him play after his operation. You could tell he had missed a season, but even with that he was dominant.

"When I went back to Cincinnati, they asked if I would recommend him, I said, 'You bet.'"

The funny thing is, Muñoz remembers the story almost exactly the same way, and he told it almost verbatim when he was inducted into the Pro Football Hall of Fame in 1998, the first player of primarily Hispanic background to be so honored.

"I won't go into details, but I knew who Forrest was," Muñoz told the crowd in Canton, Ohio. "I knew he was a Hall of Fame tackle. He was putting me through a workout. So I needed to show him that I was worthy for them to pick me. He put me through some drills and I moved along and all of a sudden he decided to pass-rush me. I wasn't sure how to react, but I reacted like any offensive lineman would react. He made a move inside, made a move outside, [and] just as he made them, I stuck both hands right into his chest and jammed him to the ground. You better believe I was scared. I extended a hand, I apologized, and he said, 'No problem.' He smiled. He goes, 'That's okay.'"

Okay doesn't quite cover it. Muñoz, born on August 19, 1958, in Ontario, California, was taken with the third pick in the 1980 draft; he

DID YOU KNOW...

The 1998 Hall of Fame class included Muñoz, defensive back Paul Krause of the Washington Redskins and Minnesota Vikings, wide receiver Tommy McDonald of the Philadelphia Eagles, linebacker Mike Singletary of the Chicago Bears, and center Dwight Stephenson of the Miami Dolphins.

became one of the greatest tackles in the history of the game. At 6'6",
278 pounds, he was so dominant as a straight-on blocker that he became
the first player elected to 11 consecutive Pro Bowls. He was All-Pro from
1981 through 1991. He was named
the NFL Offensive Lineman of the
Year in 1981, 1987, and 1988, and
he was the NFL Players Association
Lineman of the Year in 1981, 1985,
1988, and 1989. He was also named
to the NFL's 75th Anniversary team.
He was even named the NFL Man
of the Year in 1991 for his community service.

What position did Anthony Muñoz play on USC's NCAA championship baseball team in 1978?

Answers to the trivia questions
are on pages 187–189.

   In spite of the early concerns
about his injuries, Muñoz missed only three games with injuries. He
started 164 of 168 games from 1980 to 1990. He even caught seven
passes and scored four touchdowns on tackle-eligible plays. During
Muñoz's tenure, the Bengals won the AFC Central Division three
times and the AFC championship twice, although they failed to win
in two trips to the Super Bowl after the 1981 and 1988 seasons.

   Muñoz chose his son, Michael, to be his presenter into the Hall
of Fame. In his speech, Michael thanked his father for always being
there. When Muñoz took the podium, he thanked a host of family
members and friends, teachers, coaches, and teammates for their
support throughout the years. Then he explained his motivation.

   "In my second year in the NFL, I knew I wasn't motivated by the
money, I knew I wasn't motivated by the notoriety," Muñoz said in
his prepared remarks. "And I sat in my hotel room the night before
the season opener and there had to be more to playing in the NFL.
And I realized as I looked through the Scripture, that there is more
than playing in the NFL. That I was to present my body as a living
sacrifice and that was my way to worship God."

Putting the *Scholar* in Scholar–Athlete

Reggie Williams is one of the most fascinating personalities ever to have played for the Bengals. Williams, born September 19, 1954, in Flint, Michigan, overcame a hearing disability as a child to become a star athlete, a graduate of Dartmouth, a leader in community service, a politician, and a vice president of Disney's Wide World of Sports Complex.

Asked how he would like to be remembered, Williams said, "I would love to be a living example of the scholar-athlete. When I was introduced before Super Bowl XXIII… 'Starting at right outside line-backer, No. 57, Councilman Reggie Williams,' that said it all. Every politician, every parent, every teacher, every coach would love to say there's balance between athletics and scholarship. In my career, I would love to be known as…a scholar-athlete who was committed to community service.

"They have to be of equal excellence. You don't want to be a strong athlete [and a] weak scholar. You don't want to be a dim-witted great athlete. You don't want to be a worst athlete [and an] egghead. There is balance. There is a yin and yang there. There is the ability for everyone to achieve that. Someone should not underachieve in the classroom because [he's] a great athlete. Someone else should not look down his nose at athletes."

Though it seems hard to believe now, given all that Williams has accomplished, there were those who looked down their noses at him and doubted his abilities as a child growing up with a hearing disability. But he refuses to say it fueled his intense desire to succeed.

"I don't know if I would say…not being intimidated by adversity [is] the fuel by which you become successful," he said.

By any measure, Williams has been successful—even if he cannot claim to be a Super Bowl champion, a Pro Bowl player, or a Pro Football Hall of Famer. His impact was much greater and lasted longer.

In 1982, he was named the Bengals' Man of the Year, an award given to a member of the team for community service. In 1986, he received the NFL's Man of the Year award for community service. In 1987, he was one of the athletes named Sportsman of the Year by *Sports Illustrated*, honoring "athletes who care." Williams was cited for his work with the Reggie Williams Scholarship Fund (for inner-city high school students heading to college), and with the Cincinnati Speech and Hearing Center. In 2003, he was named to *Sports Illustrated*'s list of 101 Most Influential Minorities in Sports. In 2004, he was inducted into the Greater Flint Afro-American Hall of Fame. In 2006, his name was even mentioned as a possible successor to NFL commissioner Paul Tagliabue. In 2007, he was elected to the College Football Hall of Fame.

Linebacker Reggie Williams (57) was once named the Bengals Man of the Year and now is vice president of Disney's Wide World of Sports Complex.

By the Numbers

Reggie Williams: Year-by-Year Tackles

Year	Tackles	Year	Tackles	Year	Tackles
1976	106*	1982	43 (strike year)	1988	65
1977	120*	1983	90	1989	48
1978	86	1984	92*		
1979	91	1985	66	Total	1,164
1980	80	1986	96		
1981	106	1987	75	*led team	

Williams is proud of each of those honors, although he can't help but wonder if he might have been somewhat overlooked as a player because of all the honors for his community service.

"The fact that you were so well-known as a community guy... meant your on-the-field contributions were overlooked," he said.

Not by those who saw him play. After graduating from Flint Southwestern High School, Williams went to Dartmouth, where he became All–Ivy League for leading Dartmouth in tackles for three seasons. As a senior, he was named to the All-America team. After graduating from Dartmouth in 1976, he was a third-round draft choice of the Bengals.

As a rookie, Williams led the team with 106 tackles. It was the beginning of a productive career that included 1,164 tackles, 62.5 sacks, 55 passes defended, 16 fumbles forced, 22 fumbles recovered, and 16 interceptions. His 62.5 career sacks are second all-time for a Bengals player (Eddie Edwards had 83.5), and his 11 sacks in 1981 rank fourth on the Bengals' list of single-season highs.

An impassioned speech by Williams at halftime during Super Bowl XVI (which was played in Detroit, only 60 miles from Flint) helped the Bengals rally from a 20–0 deficit, but they still lost to the

San Francisco 49ers, 26–21. They lost Super Bowl XXIII to the 49ers, too, 20–16.

Those defeats were part of the reason Williams eventually left Cincinnati, in spite of becoming the first African American elected to the City Council on his first attempt, which came after he was appointed to fill a vacant seat.

Asked how he looks back on his time in Cincinnati, Williams quotes Charles Dickens from *A Tale of Two Cities*. "It was the best of times, it was the worst of times," he said. "The worst of times was losing. The best of times is the admiration from fans. Every athlete should say their fans are the best. But we had 47,000 fans who showed up when it was 59 degrees below zero [wind chill] to root us on to the AFC championship. I think they have taken the mantle of the greatest fans and those who deserve a Super Bowl championship. I loved the community and I loved the fans. I enjoyed being a Cincinnati Bengal. I still wear black and orange. But we lost two Super Bowls. We lost them to the same team. We lost them close.… We should have won both those games.

"I went into politics because I feel that everyone should have a mandatory commitment to public service. It was an opportunity to put some substance in that theory for myself, personally. I enjoyed politics. I think the media that follows the world of politics is extraordinarily petty. I also felt that there is a cultural battle going on between the sports media and the political media. So that whole issue of one-upmanship…I was under unusual scrutiny that I didn't want to subject my family to for the rest of my lifetime. It

DID YOU KNOW...

That as a senior in high school at Flint Southwestern, Reggie Williams played fullback and rushed for 100 yards in a game against Bay City?

was time to move on. So I enjoyed it, but the future had no Super Bowl wins in it.

"If you're not going to win a Super Bowl, then what's the next best thing? Well, I'm living the one better thing, and that is providing a platform for kids' dreams to come true. And that's Disney's Wide World of Sports."

The Wide World of Sports is a 200-acre sports complex that includes baseball, softball, basketball, track, soccer, tennis, and football facilities and sponsors events for more than 100,000 children every year.

Williams was asked what he learns from the athletes who visit the complex. "I learned that passion has no bounds," he said. "I also learned that even the biggest hurt can be resolved at the Magic Kingdom."

The Epitome of Toughness

In the fall of 2006, if you typed "Tim Krumrie" into the Google search engine form, the first thing that came up in the results was an entry from Wikipedia, the free online encyclopedia, which begins: "Krumrie may perhaps be best known for suffering one of the most dramatic football injuries ever televised, a shattered leg during Super Bowl XXIII…." This is before his biography as the Kansas City Chiefs' defensive line coach, or his pro football statistics. In fact, the secondary heading in Krumrie's Google results at that time read: "See results for: Tim Krumrie broken leg," and the first entry under *that* is "Most horrible sports injuries of all time."

Former Bengals defensive back Solomon Wilcots was right there as Krumrie, the Bengals' nose tackle, tried to slow up San Francisco running back Roger Craig early in Super Bowl XXIII in Miami. Krumrie's cleats caught in the grass, but the rest of his body spun around 180 degrees.

"Tim Krumrie and I both collided with Roger Craig," Wilcots recalled. "Roger Craig broke right up the middle of the defense. I was coming up to make a head-on tackle, and Tim Krumrie stuck out his leg to trip him. Tim didn't care—he'd sacrifice his body for anything. He was just trying to get the guy on the ground any way he could. He sticks his leg out and the pressure from the collision of the three of us…something had to give, and it was his leg.

"All I remember is getting up and looking up and [seeing] the scoreboard replay and thinking, 'Oh my God. He's done. He's not coming back.' I just heard him yelling. He was a tough guy. So, he wasn't yelling like I would have been yelling. But it was a nasty break. You could tell when you looked up at the big screen that he wasn't coming back. That was pretty ugly."

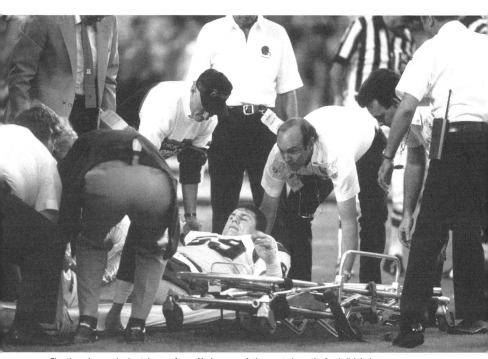

Tim Krumrie may be best known for suffering one of the most dramatic football injuries ever televised—a shattered leg during Super Bowl XXIII—but returned to play six more seasons with the Bengals.

DID YOU KNOW...

That Tim Krumrie still holds the University of Wisconsin records for career solo tackles, with 276, and career tackles by a defensive lineman, with 444?

Former Bengals wide receiver Cris Collinsworth couldn't look at the scoreboard that day. He insists he still hasn't seen a replay of the injury.

"I was probably the only one in the stadium [not to have seen it]," Collinsworth said. "He was such a good friend that I just couldn't make myself look at the Jumbotron. So much of the toughness of our football team was lost when Tim Krumrie went out of the game. He was the emotional straw of that defense."

Krumrie was taken to the locker room, but he refused to leave the stadium until he was about to go into shock. Eventually doctors discovered he had two breaks in his tibia and another in his fibula. They implanted a 15-inch steel rod in his leg, but it hardly even slowed him. He was ready to go in training camp and played six more years.

That was the most dramatic example of Krumrie's toughness, but not the only one. Anyone who played with him for any amount of time has some story to tell. Even today, as a defensive line coach for the Kansas City Chiefs, he still likes to mix it up with his players.

Writing in *The Kansas City Star*, columnist Jason Whitlock noted that Krumrie was best known for the broken leg.

"But he's also known for his tenacity as a player and as an assistant coach," Whitlock wrote. "For the Bengals, he was a 6'2", 265-pound busybody. He was a relentless pest. He wasn't bigger, faster, or stronger than anyone he played against. He was more persistent."

Krumrie learned that tenacity and persistence growing up on a dairy farm in Mondovi, Wisconsin. Born May 20, 1960, he stayed close to home, attending the University of Wisconsin, where he became a three-time All-Big Ten defensive tackle. He lasted until the 10th round of the 1983 NFL draft, when—in a stroke of genius—the Bengals made him the 276th player taken. Twelve years later, he retired with two Pro Bowl appearances, 188 games, 1,017 tackles (including 700 solos), 34.5 sacks for 238 yards in losses, 13 fumble recoveries, 11 forced fumbles, and 10 passes defended.

After a stellar playing career based on effort and technique, Krumrie spent eight more seasons as a defensive coach with the Bengals, then spent three more seasons as a defensive coach in Buffalo before moving to Kansas City in 2006. Chiefs coach Herm Edwards was thrilled to have him, and in a column written during training camp, Whitlock referred to Krumrie as the Chiefs' leading candidate for most valuable coach.

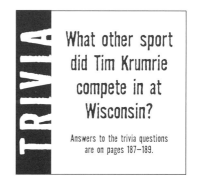

What other sport did Tim Krumrie compete in at Wisconsin?

Answers to the trivia questions are on pages 187–189.

"Krumrie, 46, doesn't look much different from his playing days," Whitlock wrote. "He's 15 pounds lighter. He still walks on his toes, which makes him look hyper or animated when he moves. And he still likes to mix it up with his players. He can demonstrate and participate in all the drills his players do."

Krumrie told Whitlock, "I coach in the grass."

Asked by Whitlock how he would get the Chiefs defensive linemen to play with the proper level of intensity, Krumrie said, "I just have to be consistent. You want the players to be a reflection of their coach. And I have to be consistent. I can't yell and scream one day and then say nothing to them the next day. We need intensity in the drills we do. I'm wide open all the time, and that's how I want them to be."

The Bengals' Other Quarterback

In the week leading up to Super Bowl XLI between the Indianapolis Colts and the Chicago Bears, Boomer Esiason's weekly column for NFL.com discussed the starting quarterbacks for each team: Peyton Manning and Rex Grossman, respectively.

Although the headline on the column read "Super Bowl may determine Peyton's place," there was an especially revealing comment with regard to Grossman, whose Bears were decided underdogs.

"As for the 'other' quarterback," Esiason wrote, "in some ways I was just like him. In Super Bowl XXIII, there was this other guy by the name of Joe Montana standing on the opposite sideline. I remember how angry we were that no one living outside of Cincinnati thought the Bengals could beat the San Francisco 49ers.

"That perceived lack of respect fueled our team and gave us the necessary nudge to stand toe-to-toe with the great Bill Walsh and the 49ers."

The Bengals did not beat the 49ers that day. Montana completed 23 of 36 passes for 357 yards and two touchdowns, including a 10-yard scoring pass to John Taylor with just 34 seconds left. San Francisco rallied past Cincinnati, 20–16, in what is widely regarded as one of the most exciting Super Bowls.

Esiason had been great all season. In fact, he had been voted the league's Most Valuable Player that year after completing 223 of 388 passes for 3,572 yards and 28 touchdowns. His quarterback rating in the regular season was 97.4.

But in the Super Bowl, he completed just 11 of 25 passes for 144 yards. He had no touchdowns and one interception. Still, he thought that might be enough after Jim Breech kicked a 40-yard field goal to put Cincinnati ahead, 16–13, with 3:20 left.

"After Jimmy kicked that, with the way our defense was playing, I figured this was going to be a sweet ride home," Esiason told reporters after the game. But Montana and the 49ers had other ideas.

"I think that what Joe did at the end, you might as well forget about the great Denver drive [against the Browns] that got them into the Super Bowl," Esiason said. "It's now the great San Francisco drive that won them the Super Bowl."

Despite that loss, however, Esiason remains one of the most popular players ever to wear a Bengals jersey, a left-handed gunslinger who presided over some of the franchise's glory years before being traded to the New York Jets in 1993. In fact, he was so popular the Bengals even brought him back a second time, in 1997, before he decided to retire and go into broadcasting.

He ranks in the top 15 in NFL history with 37,920 passing yards, 2,969 completions, 5,205 attempts, and 247 touchdown passes. For

By the Numbers

Boomer Esiason's Career Passing Statistics

Year	Team	Games	Comp	Att	Pct.	Yards	Avg.	TD	INT
1984	Cin	10	51	102	50.0	530	5.2	3	3
1985	Cin	15	251	431	58.2	3443	8.0	27	12
1986	Cin	16	273	469	58.2	3959	8.4	24	17
1987	Cin	12	240	440	54.5	3321	7.5	16	19
1988	Cin	16	223	388	57.5	3572	9.2	28	14
1989	Cin	16	258	455	56.7	3525	7.7	28	11
1990	Cin	16	224	402	55.7	3031	7.5	24	22
1991	Cin	14	233	413	56.4	2883	7.0	13	16
1992	Cin	12	144	278	51.8	1407	5.1	11	15
1993	NYJ	16	288	473	60.9	3421	7.2	16	11
1994	NYJ	15	255	440	58.0	2782	6.3	17	13
1995	NYJ	12	221	389	56.8	2275	5.8	16	15
1996	Ari	10	190	339	56.0	2293	6.8	11	14
1997	Cin	7	118	186	63.4	1478	7.9	13	2
Totals		187	2,969	5,205	57.0	37,920	7.3	247	184

the Bengals, he's second only to Ken Anderson in almost every career category, including attempts, completions, yards, touchdowns, and interceptions.

Former Bengals receiver turned broadcaster Cris Collinsworth played with Anderson and Esiason.

"Complete opposites," Collinsworth said when asked to compare the two. "Boomer was the showman. He was the Mad Bomber. He was the guy who would wind up and throw it. It was like catching a Nolan Ryan fastball. They were catchable if you had the hands to catch them. They were as hard as any quarterback I've ever seen or played for. He also had a charisma and a flair to him that was unmatched in anybody I'd ever played with. It was exciting to be in the huddle with him.

"Both of them won the MVP. Both of them took us to the Super Bowl. They did it on completely different paths. Both were exciting, great quarterbacks with very different styles."

TRIVIA

What's Boomer Esiason's real first name?

Answers to the trivia questions are on pages 187–189.

Esiason was born April 17, 1961, in West Islip, New York. His mother, who gave him the nickname "Boomer" because of the way he kicked while she was pregnant, died of cancer when he was just a boy, so he was raised by his father and two sisters.

After an outstanding collegiate career at the University of Maryland—where he set 17 school records on offense, was named an All-American, and took the Terrapins to an ACC title and the 1983 Citrus Bowl—Esiason was shocked when he was not a first-round pick in the 1984 NFL draft. When the Bengals took him in the second round with the 38th pick overall, he became the first quarterback taken that day. But, obviously, it was not the same as being a first-round selection. Some think the snub is what fueled Esiason's intensity.

The young Esiason had the advantage of being brought along slowly behind the wily veteran Anderson. After the Bengals lost the first five games of the 1984 season, Esiason made his first start on October 7, leading Cincinnati to a 13–3 victory over Houston. He did not become the Bengals' regular starter until September 22, 1985, but Dan Fouts led the San Diego Chargers to a 44–41 victory that day. Nevertheless, from that day forward, Esiason was the man in Cincinnati.

He and Wyche instilled new life into the franchise, which had its ups and downs after a Super Bowl appearance following the 1981 season. One of the low points came in 1987, when the Bengals struggled to a 4–11 record in a season interrupted by a players' strike. Esiason was the team's player representative, a tough job for a young player on a bad team.

But then came the 1988 season—and another Super Bowl appearance—and all was forgiven.

Unfortunately, Esiason and the Bengals were unable to duplicate that season. But he continued to have productive seasons until 1992, when Dave Shula replaced Wyche as Bengals head coach and David Klingler replaced Esiason as the Bengals quarterback.

In 1993, Esiason was traded to the New York Jets. That season he had career highs in attempts, with 473; completions, with 288; and completion percentage, with 60.9 percent, resulting in his fourth trip to the Pro Bowl. After two more seasons in New York, Esiason signed with the Arizona Cardinals as a free agent in 1996 before closing out his career back in Cincinnati. In 1997, Esiason completed 118 of 186 passes for 1,478 yards and 13 touchdowns, a quarterback rating of 106.9. On the final play of his career, he threw a 77-yard touchdown pass to Darnay Scott.

He left the Bengals to join ABC's *Monday Night Football* tele-cast, marking the start of a long and successful broadcasting career. In addition, he and his wife, Cheryl, are involved in numerous charitable activities through the Boomer Esiason Foundation, formed to help find a cure for cystic fibrosis. The Esiasons' son, Gunnar, was diagnosed with the disease in 1993. In 1995, Esiason received the Walter Payton Man of the Year Award for his charitable work.

Dancing with the Stars

Ickey Woods doesn't remember saying it, but he has heard it enough that he doesn't doubt he did.

The former Bengals star, who is now the coach of the Cincinnati Sizzle in the National Women's Football Association, told his players they could not dance in the end zone after scoring.

That's right. The creator of the Ickey Shuffle has pulled the plug on happy feet.

"They claim I told them they couldn't do an end zone shuffle," a laughing Woods said. "I don't remember saying that, but they said I did. I've got five or six people telling me I said it, so I must have."

The irony is not lost on the former Bengals running back. Almost 20 years after his rookie year with the Bengals, people still stop him on the street and ask him to do the dance he made famous, a dance that became so popular Bengals founder Paul Brown reportedly did his own version.

"It's my legacy," Woods said. "Everywhere I go people want to see the Ickey Shuffle. But I have to tell them I'm getting older now. I'm 40 years old. I don't do the shuffle no more. It's something I did when I was in my early 20s."

It's almost impossible to believe that Woods's entire NFL career spanned just four seasons.

From a thrill-filled rookie season that culminated in a Super Bowl appearance, through a series of knee injuries, he played just 37 games with the Bengals. But he remains as closely affiliated with the franchise as almost anybody—all because of that dance. Bengals fans can still see him hopping on his left foot, then his right, then spiking the ball, twirling his finger, and swiveling his hips while yelling, "Woo! Woo! Woo!"

The only problem was that those knee injuries prevented him from doing the dance as long as he—and the fans—would have liked.

Woods, born February 28, 1966, in Fresno, California, led the nation in rushing yards per carry his senior year at the University of Nevada–Las Vegas. In spite of that, he wasn't selected until the Bengals claimed him in the second round of the 1988 draft.

His impact was felt immediately. He carried the ball 203 times for 1,066 yards and 15 touchdowns, which ranked him second in the league in rushing touchdowns and tied for second in total touchdowns. He also caught 21

TRIVIA

What's Ickey Woods's real first name?

Answers to the trivia questions are on pages 187–189.

passes for 199 more yards, averaging 5.3 yards per carry and 9.5 yards per reception.

In playoff victories over Seattle and Buffalo, he had 52 carries for 228 yards and three touchdowns. He had 20 carries for 79 yards in Super Bowl XXIII, but he did not score in the Bengals' 20–16 loss.

In the second game of the 1989 season, a 41–10 victory over Pittsburgh, Woods tore his left anterior cruciate ligament and missed the rest of the season. In 1990, Harold Green had taken over his starting job, but Woods played 10 games, rushing for 268 yards. He did have a touchdown in the Bengals' 41–14 playoff victory over Houston. Then he injured his right knee in the 1991 preseason. He

Ickey Woods celebrated his touchdowns with the famous Ickey Shuffle.

wound up playing just nine games, rushing for just 97 yards on 36 carries. He retired after the season, with a total of 332 carries for 1,525 yards and 27 touchdowns.

Asked how he viewed his career, Woods said, "I've got to be satisfied. I played four years. I wish I could have played longer, but injuries took me away from the game. That's part of the game, so you've got to take the good with the bad and roll with it. You can't cry about it. It's not going to do anybody any good. I don't reminisce about the past. I just move to the future."

His future now includes coaching his sons, Jovante and Aubrhee, as well as the Sizzle. He got involved coaching women when his ex-wife, Chandra, decided to try out for the team.

"I sarcastically said to her that if she made the team and they needed help coaching, I'd help coach," Woods said. "I didn't realize she would come home and say, 'Honey, guess what? They need a coach.'

"I took it on four years ago and it has been good for me. I had a chance to sit back and see that women do have the talent to play football. There really are some talented women out there. It has been a blessing to be able to coach these women because they love to play the game of football."

Woods said he tried to pattern himself after his running back coach in college, John Montgomery.

"I use a lot of his philosophy in my coaching style," Woods said. "He's the one who got me over the hump and got me to the NFL. A lot of the stuff he taught me I try to instill in the women and kids I'm coaching now."

He has found that there's a big difference coaching women.

"The mentality is different," he said. "Women are a little more timid. You can't yell at them like you do when you're coaching a men's team. I can yell and cuss and rant and rave at my men's team and tomorrow it's okay. They don't take it home with them. But women seem to hold onto it a little longer and bring it to practice the next day. It takes them a lot longer to get over it than the men, so you have to have a much different approach.

"You have to be patient. I put them in the same boat as the youth football teams I coach. You have to be a lot more patient. They really don't know the game of football; they were not raised playing football like men are. Men think they know it all. But women are like sponges. They absorb it a lot better than the men do."

By the Numbers

Ickey Woods's Rushing Statistics

1988: 16 games, 203 carries, 1,066 yards, 15 touchdowns
1989: Two games, 29 carries, 94 yards, two touchdowns
1990: 10 games, 64 carries, 268 yards, six touchdowns
1991: Nine games, 36 carries, 97 yards, four touchdowns
Totals: 37 games, 332 carries, 1,525 yards, 27 touchdowns

The Sizzle, playing at LaSalle High School, went 2–6 in their first season and 3–5 in their second. Woods knows his name is a draw—but once fans see how hard the women work, they tend to come back again and again.

"Winning curcs all ills," Woods said. "If we can win on a consistent basis, then that will put some butts in the stands."

And if that doesn't work, maybe he can teach them the Ickey Shuffle.

Playing It Safe-ty

Solomon Wilcots enjoyed almost every minute of his four seasons with the Bengals.

"It was wonderful," the popular broadcaster said when asked how he looked back on his career as a defensive back with Cincinnati from 1987 to 1990.

The only two downers he recalled were the NFL players' strike his first season and the Bengals' loss to Joe Montana and the San Francisco 49ers in the Super Bowl the next season.

Still, for an eighth-round draft pick out of the University of Colorado who was switched from cornerback to safety, Wilcots doesn't have many complaints.

"I remember when I was at the University of Colorado and I got the call from [defensive coordinator/defensive backs coach] Dick LeBeau saying, 'We selected you to come play in our secondary,'" said Wilcots, who played cornerback in college and was All–Big Eight as a senior. "They had drafted three other guys before me to play in the secondary, including Eric Thomas, a good friend of mine. We had worked out and roomed together at the NFL Combine. There were two safeties—Leonard Bell and Sonny Gordon from Big Ten schools [Indiana and Ohio State, respectively].

"I remember in my first mini-camp, coach Sam Wyche said to me, 'You're going to be given a chance to make this team. Don't look at where you were drafted. You're going to be given a chance to make this team.' That's all anyone can hope for. I think they understood that maybe I was more deserving than that 'eighth-round' tag. Even Paul Brown came over to talk to me. I was very encouraged that I could stick."

Wilcots worked his tail off and made the team. Two weeks into the regular season, the players went on strike.

"It was an inauspicious start," Wilcots recalled, laughing.

Actually, the week before the strike wasn't too great, either. The Bengals played host to the 49ers. Cincinnati built a big lead but the 49ers came back and won the game, 27–26.

"I was like, 'What the hell just happened?'" Wilcots said. "I'm a wide-eyed rookie thinking, 'We had that team beat.' I remember Dick LeBeau saying, 'In college, you get that kind of lead and teams quit. But not in the NFL. You play until the last whistle.'"

Wilcots took that lesson to heart and returned with a vengeance when the players' strike ended in mid-October. The Bengals struggled that season, finishing 4–11. But Wilcots didn't let up. When LeBeau suggested he learn to play safety, he embraced the new position. After the Bengals' last game of the season, a 21–17 loss at Houston in which Wilcots picked off his first interception (against Warren Moon, no less), LeBeau approached him.

"Dick LeBeau came up to Eric Thomas and I and said, 'I want you two to go home [and] work out as hard as you can. Because from the day we arrive at training camp, you're taking every snap in my secondary,'" Wilcots said.

Wilcots and Thomas did just that and came back raring to go.

"I remember the first day of camp, Paul Brown always addressed us," Wilcots said. "He said, 'I don't really know what to say to you except to say that every team you play is scared to death of you. They don't know what team is going to show up—the team they played in the first half of last year that can beat anybody, or the team that played in the second half of last year that allowed anyone to beat them. If you guys just show up and play and believe you can win, there's no telling how far you can go.'

"I remember thinking, 'This old man can still coach.' You could hear a pin drop. It was clear to everyone in the room why he was a Hall of Famer. You didn't have to question it. The guy could still coach. To his dying day, he still had it. And he was so right. We got off to a 6–0 start. We were part of the zone blitz defense that Dick LeBeau introduced. We go to the Super Bowl. And lo and behold, history repeats itself and Joe Montana brings the 49ers back and they beat us again, just like in my rookie season."

Though losing to the 49ers, 20–16, in Super Bowl XXIII was bad enough, Wilcots still can't forget one play.

"It sticks in my craw even to tell this," he admitted. "Remember, I was in my first year playing safety. We had a guy who is now the defensive backfield coach for the Pittsburgh Steelers—Ray Horton. He was a veteran guy who had played safety. He helped me learn how to play the position. I'm grateful to Ray Horton. During the week we had practiced this coverage—Double Rice. When Jerry Rice was in the slot, the cornerback would have him on any outside cut. The safety would have him on any inside cut in the middle of the field. I remember picking passes off during the week of practice. I was thinking, 'Man, if we call that play, I'm going to be a hero. I'm going to be the man.' You play the game out in your mind so many times before you get out there.

"So we get in the game, we get the 49ers in second-and-25. We're getting ready to run our play, right? The next thing I know, Ray Horton's coming in for me. I know Dick LeBeau wanted the veteran in there. So San Francisco runs the play we think they're going to run.

After switching from cornerback to free safety,
Solomon Wilcots started two of his final
three seasons with the Bengals.
Who started at free safety in 1989?

Answers to the trivia questions
are on pages 187–189.

Dick LeBeau's a genius. He called the right defensive play. Well, Ray Horton, God bless his soul, misses Jerry Rice. He collides with Eric Thomas, our corner. All three of our guys collide. Jerry Rice goes running down the field. Rickey Dixon makes a touchdown-saving tackle, but Rice picks up the first down. In the zone blitz defense, you salivate when you get a team second-and-long or third-and-long. Second-and-25? Oh, that's a big play waiting to happen, a touchdown for the defense.

"So I'm pissed off. I don't talk to anyone. I don't talk to my coaches. I don't talk to my teammates. I go home for the off-season. I can't sleep for two months after that game. Ray Horton goes to Dallas and he gets a Super Bowl ring in Dallas. I'm still sitting here without one. That's what I remember from that game. I'm not blaming anyone. I'm not criticizing. I'm just telling you that was going to be my moment and it never happened."

Wilcots is laughing at himself as he finishes the story. In spite of failing to win a Super Bowl, the Bengals of that era taught Wilcots a lot.

"My fondest thing about that time, and I didn't notice it then but I see it now, is how…cutting-edge that team was," he said. "It's clear what [general manager] Paul Brown had put together. We had a coach in Sam Wyche who put in the no-huddle offense that [Buffalo coach] Marv Levy tried to get outlawed for the AFC championship game.

By the Numbers

Players Who Have Worn No. 41 for the Bengals

White Graves, 1968
Terry Swanson, 1969
Dave Green, 1974–75
Sam Washington, 1985
Solomon Wilcots, 1987–90
Joe King, 1991
Forey Duckett (Games 1–2), 1994

Adrian Hardy (Game 3), 1994
Scottie Graham, 1997
Lorenzo Neal, 2001–02
Chris Edmonds, 2003
Patrick Body, 2005
Chinedum Ndukwe, 2007

"The morning of the championship game Marv Levy called NFL commissioner Paul Tagliabue and told him it was illegal. For a moment, they were contemplating not letting us use it. The league had to meet.

"Sam Wyche told us they were running scared and that we may not be able to use it but we were going to kick their asses anyway. We're waiting on a call from the league office to see if we could use our no-huddle offense. So we get the call. We use it. We beat them, 21–10. Then the next year, guess who's using the no-huddle offense?"

After losing the Super Bowl, the Bengals went 8–8 in 1989 and 9–7 in 1990, losing to Bo Jackson and the Raiders, 20–10, in the AFC divisional playoff game at Los Angeles on January 13, 1991.

"I wanted badly to win that game," Wilcots said. "I remember thinking, 'I have just played my last game as a Cincinnati Bengal.' I just knew. I knew the business of it and how they were operating and knew I would have an opportunity. I was going to take it because I felt we weren't improving as a team."

Plan B free agency had come to the league, and the Bengals decided to take a chance and leave Wilcots unprotected. They knew he had strong ties to the community and they thought he wouldn't look to leave. But they were wrong. He signed with Minnesota, playing one season with the Vikings, and then reunited with LeBeau in Pittsburgh for one season before retiring. His career had spanned six seasons, and he played in every game his final five years.

Wilcots, born October 9, 1964, in Los Angeles, grew up in Compton and then attended Rubidoux High School in Riverside. The son of a minister, he read all the classics and became an English-literature major at Colorado, which comes in handy when he is writing columns for NFL.com along with his broadcasting duties for CBS, the NFL Network, and Sirius NFL Radio. He still lives in Cincinnati with his wife and three children.

Chapter Six

Super Bowl Dreams

Ten Great Games (Not in the Super Bowl)

What makes a football game great?

A victory? An amazing individual performance? Memorable circumstances? Can a regular-season game in a losing year be great, or must it be a playoff game with the added pressure it brings?

Obviously, there are no right answers. Each fan comes to each game with his or her own expectations and leaves with his or her own reactions to what transpired. But here's a list of 10 great Bengals games that won't soon be forgotten by those who saw them.

November 15, 1970, at Riverfront Stadium: Cincinnati 14, Cleveland 10. Although Cincinnati beat visiting Cleveland in the preseason, this was the first time the Bengals had beaten the Browns in the regular season, and the 60,007 fans in attendance roared their approval. There was no denying what the victory meant to coach Paul Brown, the architect of both teams, who had been unceremoniously dumped by Cleveland owner Art Modell after the 1962 season. Wrote the normally staid Brown in his autobiography, "When I ran off the field following our 14–10 victory, I took off my hat and waved it to the crowd—something I don't even remember doing—because I was so exhilarated at our victory over a team with better talent and deeper resources. I can't recall our team's ever fighting harder against great odds than in this game.

"The turning point was our defense's stopping the Browns inside our 10-yard line in the first quarter and forcing them to kick a field goal for a 10–0 lead when a touchdown might have pushed the game out of control. We scored twice in the second half, keyed by Willie Lee Jones's sack of Mike Phipps that began our comeback, and our defense battled for its life to hold that lead. One of my friends told me afterward that I looked as if I were eighteen years old the way I ran off the field, and I told him, 'That's exactly how I felt.' I confess to having tears in my eyes when our players handed me the game ball."

December 20, 1970, at Riverfront Stadium: Cincinnati 45, Boston 7. It was an historic day for the young Bengals and the 60,157 fans in attendance. In the first season after the NFL/AFL merger and thus the first with the new conference and division configurations, the team became the first AFC Central Division champions. In addition, the Bengals qualified for the playoffs in just their third season, the fastest an expansion team had managed to do so at the time. A triumphant Paul Brown was carried off the field by his players. That photograph is reproduced on the cover of his autobiography.

November 17, 1975, at Riverfront Stadium: Cincinnati 33, Buffalo 24. Ken Anderson upstaged O.J. Simpson on one of football's biggest stages—*Monday Night Football*. Simpson was especially elusive, running for 197 yards, but Anderson passed for 447 yards, much to the delight of the crowd of 56,666 in Cincinnati's Riverfront Stadium.

"He was unreal," Simpson said of Anderson.

"He's cool, efficient, the best we've ever played," added Buffalo defensive end Walt Patulski.

November 20, 1977, at Riverfront Stadium: Cincinnati 23, Miami 17. Tight end Bob Trumpy had quite a career for the Bengals, especially considering he was a 12th-round draft choice, the 301st player taken overall in the team's first collegiate draft in 1968. He was named to the Pro Bowl in 1968, 1969, 1970, and 1973. His career was coming to a close in 1977, when he had just 18 receptions for 251 yards and one touchdown. But he still gets asked about that one touchdown, a 29-yard flea flicker from Anderson in a driving rainstorm that knocked the Dolphins out of the playoff picture. Anderson handed off to running back Archie Griffin, who pitched the ball to receiver John McDaniel on a reverse. Then McDaniel gave

TRIVIA

Who holds the record for most points scored for the Bengals in a single game?

Answers to the trivia questions are on pages 187–189.

it back to Anderson, who threw it to Trumpy. Twenty years later, Trumpy seemed surprised to be asked yet again about the play, which was called "triple pass."

"How did you know that's what it was called?" he said, laughing. "I scored a lot on that. When I retired and began work for NBC, for 20 years after I retired, every time I saw Don Shula, Shula would say to me, 'I still remember that damn reverse pass in the rain.' For 20 years I told him, 'We called it triple pass, Coach.' He'd always say, 'Yeah, I know. I know.' So I was reminded of that a lot."

September 6, 1981, at Riverfront Stadium: Cincinnati 27, Seattle 21. This might have been the most memorable game in Turk Schonert's career—and a heck of a way to start it off. As a senior at Stanford, Schonert led the NCAA in passing efficiency with a rating of 164.5. He also led the Pac-10 conference in touchdowns with 19, but he was just a ninth-round draft choice of the Chicago Bears in 1980 and didn't even make the team. In 1981, he was a rookie with the Bengals, the third quarterback behind Anderson and Jack Thompson.

In the opening game of the 1981 season, Anderson threw two interceptions as the Seahawks built a 21–0 lead in the first quarter. Coach Forrest Gregg benched Anderson for the second half, and since Thompson was injured, Schonert got the nod. He brought the Bengals back, completing nine of 18 passes for 130 yards. Pete Johnson scored two touchdowns, and Jim Breech kicked two field goals.

The game was a blip in each quarterback's career. Anderson went on to have the best season of his career and win the NFL's MVP award while leading the Bengals to Super Bowl XVI. He threw only eight interceptions in the remaining 15 games of the season. In nine seasons with Cincinnati and Atlanta, Schonert played in 72 games, many as a holder for place kicks. In his career, he completed 311 of 504 passes for 3,788 yards, 11 touchdowns, and 20 interceptions. He was 7–5 in 12 career starts. He went on to coach with Tampa Bay, Buffalo, Carolina, the New York Giants, and New Orleans.

January 10, 1982, at Riverfront Stadium: Cincinnati 27, San Diego 7. Gregg was a player in the infamous Ice Bowl in Green Bay in 1967, when the temperature was minus 13 as the Packers beat the Dallas Cowboys in the NFL Championship game. But this game was colder. The temperature was minus 9, with a wind chill of minus 59, which is believed to be the coldest game played in NFL history. There were 13,277 no-shows, but the 46,302 who showed up for what became known as the "Freezer Bowl" were treated to the Bengals' first AFC championship game. "I told them that there was nothing we could do about the weather and that we had to fight through it," Gregg said of his players. "I thought they did a super job. Guys like Ken Anderson, Pete Johnson, and Blair Bush, our center who had to handle the ball so much, did so well. The whole team showed mental toughness. It was a great job."

Said San Diego coach Don Coryell, "It was very, very windy in the first quarter, but that's no excuse. We were just beaten. Give them credit for hanging onto the football." San Diego, which came into the game with the best offense in the league, lost the ball on two fumbles and two interceptions.

December 17, 1989, at Riverfront Stadium: Cincinnati 61, Houston 7. After running up the score, coach Sam Wyche made no secret of his dislike for the Oilers and their coach, Jerry Glanville, who—not surprisingly—did not shake Wyche's hand after the game.

"I don't like their team and I don't like their people," Wyche told reporters after the game. "I wish today was a five-quarter game. If they did not make as many dumb mistakes, they would win a lot more football games. You can only be so stupid, and they have exceeded the limit. That is a team with no discipline. And when you don't have discipline, you have a hard time winning.... We were going right for the jugular, and we weren't going to rest on our heels, either. They are so obnoxious. They are such an obnoxious team. They think they're cute, but they're silly.... Jerry Glanville is probably the biggest phony in professional football. I don't like people who are phonies."

Glanville declined to respond to Wyche's comments other than to say, "Our job is to stop them. All I can do is coach our team."

DID YOU KNOW...

That the Bengals have won three games without scoring a touchdown? On September 24, 1972, Horst Muhlmann kicked five field goals as the Bengals beat the visiting Pittsburgh Steelers, 15–10. On October 21, 1984, Jim Breech kicked four field goals as the Bengals beat the visiting Cleveland Browns, 12–9. On November 6, 1994, Doug Pelfrey kicked a club-record six field goals and linebacker/defensive end Alfred Williams added a safety as the Bengals won at Seattle, 20–17, in overtime.

By the Numbers

Score by Quarters in 61–7 Rout of Houston

Houston	0	0	0	7	7
Cincinnati	21	10	21	9	61

November 16, 2003, at Paul Brown Stadium: Cincinnati 24, Kansas City 19. If there was one game that signaled a change in the football fortunes of Cincinnati, this might be it. Kansas City came into the game with a 9–0 record, the only remaining undefeated team in the league. Cincinnati, which had the worst record of any NFL team between 1991 and 2002, was 4–5 under new coach Marvin Lewis. Nonetheless, outspoken wide receiver Chad Johnson had guaranteed a Bengals victory, and his teammates made good on his promise. Peter Warrick scored two touchdowns, Rudi Johnson ran for 165 yards, and Jon Kitna threw two touchdown passes for the Bengals. "From the time we started, we said we were going to bring the NFL back here. And that was NFL football out there today," Lewis said.

October 25, 2004, at Paul Brown Stadium: Cincinnati 23, Denver 10. It had been 12 years since the Bengals played on *Monday Night Football* and 15 since *Monday Night Football* was staged in Cincinnati. That explained why a crowd of 65,806—the biggest ever to see a Bengals game in Cincinnati—turned out to watch the 1–4 Bengals host the 5–1 Broncos, whose defense was ranked number one in the NFL. Chad Johnson caught seven passes for 149 yards. He had two 50-yard catches, one for a touchdown, against Denver cornerback Champ Bailey. Rudi Johnson ran for 119 yards, including a 36-yard touchdown. It was only the second time all season that an opponent had scored so many points on Denver's defense.

November 28, 2004, at Paul Brown Stadium: Cincinnati 58, Cleveland 48. Rudi Johnson rushed for a career-high 202 yards and two touchdowns, including the go-ahead score, in the highest-scoring game since the NFL-AFL merger in 1970. Carson Palmer threw four touchdown passes and three interceptions in a wild game that saw Cincinnati squander a 14-point lead before rallying to win.

The victory made up for a 34–17 loss to the Browns at Cleveland on October 17 in what had become known as the Pepto-Bismol game. The week before the game, Chad Johnson sent the Browns defensive backs bottles of Pepto-Bismol, insinuating that they'd get sick trying to cover him. But Johnson had just three catches for 37 yards in that game. In this game, he had 10 catches for 117 yards.

It was the fifth straight loss for the Browns, and coach Butch Davis resigned the next day, citing "intense pressure and scrutiny" in a statement he released to the media.

The 1981 Super Bowl Season

The most successful Bengals season ever came up one victory short. Forrest Gregg and his Cincinnati team lost Super Bowl XVI to the San Francisco 49ers, 26–21, in Pontiac, Michigan, on January 24, 1982. Here's a look at that memorable season, game-by-game.

September 6, in Cincinnati: Cincinnati 27, Seattle 21. Pete Johnson had 20 carries for 84 yards and two touchdowns and became the Bengals' all-time leading rusher with 3,071 yards as the Bengals rallied for victory.

September 13, at New York: Cincinnati 31, New York Jets 30. Ken Anderson's three-yard touchdown pass to Archie Griffin with 3:34 left, and defensive end Mike St. Clair's fumble recovery and 12-yard touchdown run 31 seconds later, allowed the Bengals to rally for the second time in two weeks.

September 20, in Cincinnati: Cleveland 20, Cincinnati 17. The Browns dominated offensively, running 81 plays to 40 for the Bengals and holding the ball for 42 minutes, compared to just 18 for the Bengals. Cincinnati's troubles were compounded when Jim Breech missed one field goal and had another blocked by Hanford Dixon.

September 27, in Cincinnati: Cincinnati 27, Buffalo 24, in overtime. Breech kicked a 28-yard field goal with 5:27 left to play in overtime. "I don't see how anybody can boo him now," Cincinnati coach Forrest Gregg said of Breech, who'd struggled the previous week.

October 4, at Houston: Houston 17, Cincinnati 10. Houston's Carl Roaches ran 96 yards with a kickoff return, and Tony Fritsch kicked a 48-yard field goal with 4:48 left, after cornerback Greg Stemrick intercepted a pass by Anderson as the Oilers rallied to win.

October 11, at Baltimore: Cincinnati 41, Baltimore 19. Anderson completed 21 of 27 passes for 257 yards and three touchdowns against a porous Baltimore defense.

October 18, in Cincinnati: Cincinnati 34, Pittsburgh 7. Anderson threw for 346 yards, but the Bengals defense stole the show as Cincinnati took over sole possession of first place in the AFC Central. The Steelers entered the game with the top-ranked rushing attack in the NFL but managed just 65 yards. "What have I played, 12 years?" said Steelers quarterback Terry Bradshaw, who completed 14 of 27 throws for 150 yards and a touchdown. "I can't remember playing in a game like this in my life where we have been so totally dominated."

October 25, at New Orleans: New Orleans 17, Cincinnati 7. The tone of the game was set when Saints linebacker Jim Kovach recovered a fumble by Johnson on the Bengals' first possession of the game. The Saints didn't capitalize then, but built a 17–0 lead later. "This game was settled on the first drive," Gregg told reporters.

The 49ers sealed their victory in the 1982 Super Bowl with a brilliant third-quarter goal-line stand; Three times they denied Bengal attempts to score from the 1.

November 1, in Cincinnati: Cincinnati 34, Houston 21. The Bengals scored 10 points in less than two minutes before halftime for a 24–7 lead that broke the game open. Anderson hit 21 of 30 passes for 281 yards and three scores. "He's like a heat-seeking missile," tight end Dan Ross told reporters after the game.

November 8, at San Diego: Cincinnati 40, San Diego 17. Cornerback Louis Breeden had quite a day, with two interceptions and a fumble recovery. He returned his first interception of the season 102 yards for a touchdown, tying an NFL record, as the Bengals pounded the Chargers. San Diego fumbled four times, losing three of them. Quarterback Dan Fouts was sacked six times in addition to throwing the two interceptions.

Bengals Starting Lineups in Super Bowl XVI

Offense		Defense	
WR	Cris Collinsworth	LE	Eddie Edwards
LT	Anthony Muñoz	NT	Wilson Whitley
LG	Dave Lapham	RE	Ross Browner
C	Blair Bush	LOLB	Bo Harris
RG	Max Montoya	LILB	Jim LeClair
RT	Mike Wilson	RILB	Glenn Cameron
TE	Dan Ross	ROLB	Reggie Williams
WR	Isaac Curtis	LCB	Louis Breeden
QB	Ken Anderson	RCB	Ken Riley
RB	Charles Alexander	SS	Bobby Kemp
FB	Pete Johnson	FS	Bryan Hicks

November 15, in Cincinnati: Cincinnati 24, Los Angeles 10. Johnson ran for two touchdowns and caught a three-yard pass from Anderson for a third score. Cincinnati picked off three of Dan Pastorini's passes to set up their touchdowns. Pastorini, making his second start with the Rams, was sacked five times. Breeden, who had two interceptions and a fumble recovery at San Diego, had two more interceptions against the Rams.

November 22, in Cincinnati: Cincinnati 38, Denver 21. Denver came into the game ranked number one in defense overall and number one against the pass. All Anderson did was complete 25 of 37 passes for 396 yards and three touchdowns.

November 29, at Cleveland: Cincinnati 41, Cleveland 21. The Bengals avenged a 20–17 loss on September 20 and mathematically eliminated the Browns from the playoff picture. Cleveland lost three fumbles, and Cincinnati turned them into touchdowns. Browns quarterback Brian Sipe was sacked five times and was knocked out of the game in the fourth quarter after the fifth sack.

December 6, at Cincinnati: San Francisco 21, Cincinnati 3. Anderson went into the game as the top-ranked quarterback in the NFL and he left the game on crutches after hyperextending his right big toe. Before the injury, he threw two interceptions and the Bengals fumbled four times. Jack Thompson, who replaced Anderson, also threw an interception. "You don't win many football games with six turnovers," Gregg said. The Bengals' five-game winning streak came to a halt, and they missed a chance to clinch a playoff spot. Joe Montana threw for two touchdowns and ran for another for San Francisco.

December 13, at Pittsburgh: Cincinnati 17, Pittsburgh 10. Anderson recovered from his hyperextended right big toe to throw two touchdown passes as the Bengals won the AFC Central Division for the first time since 1973 and earned their first trip to the playoffs since Paul Brown retired in 1975.

Brown hired Gregg in 1980. Both men had been fired by the Browns. "He was just the right man for us," Brown said of Gregg. "He gave us strong leadership. I'm glad I went ahead and got him. He's a man's man." Said Anderson of the victory and the playoff spot, "I wish you all could experience how I'm feeling now. I wish I were able to describe it. This is simply great. This has helped me forget a lot of bad memories…. A very good head coach has done a lot for us."

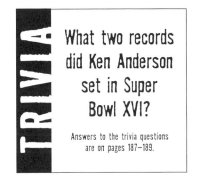

TRIVIA.

What two records did Ken Anderson set in Super Bowl XVI?

Answers to the trivia questions are on pages 187–189.

December 20, at Atlanta: Cincinnati 30, Atlanta 28. Anderson threw two touchdown passes, including one for 74 yards to Cris Collinsworth, as the Bengals finished the season with a 12–4 record, the best in the American Football Conference, which assured them of home-field advantage throughout the AFC playoffs.

DID YOU KNOW...

That Cincinnati outgained San Francisco in Super Bowl XVI, 356–275, the first time the losing team had more yards from scrimmage?

January 3, in Cincinnati: Cincinnati 28, Buffalo 21. Anderson passed for 192 yards and a touchdown as the Bengals won a playoff game for the first time in four tries. "Anderson was outstanding, but he has been all season," Gregg said. "We played a great team, and we played very well. Now we've got to be sure to keep it going. I don't care who we get next. I'm just glad to be playing somebody, to be going to work again tomorrow." Buffalo had the ball at the Bengals' 20 with a fourth-and-3 with 2:58 left, but a delay-of-game penalty wiped out a six-yard pass from Joe Ferguson to Lou Piccone that would have given the Bills a first down.

January 10, in Cincinnati: Cincinnati 27, San Diego 7. The Bengals built a 10–0 lead midway through the first quarter on a frigid day in Riverfront Stadium and handily beat San Diego for the AFC title and a trip to the Super Bowl. The Chargers, the top offensive team in the NFL, lost two fumbles and threw two interceptions.

January 24, Super Bowl XVI in Pontiac, Michigan: San Francisco 26, Cincinnati 21. The Bengals committed three turnovers in the first half and trailed at halftime, 20–0, but recovered to make a game of it. Montana completed 14 of 22 passes for 157 yards and one touchdown. He also ran for a touchdown and was named the MVP of Super Bowl XVI. Ray Wersching tied a Super Bowl record with four field goals. Said Walsh, the former Bengals assistant, "Joe Montana did a superb job. He will be the great quarterback of the future.... We deserve to be in this position. We are the best team."

Anderson completed 25 of 34 passes for 300 yards and two touchdowns, but he also threw two interceptions. Tight end Dan

Ross tied a Super Bowl record with 11 receptions. "We were loose all week and loose in the locker room before the game," Ross said. "Then we went out on the field and seemed to get stage fright. It was like we just realized that we were in the Super Bowl and all those people were here to see the game and all those millions were watching on television. It wasn't until the second half that we began to play as we are capable of playing. It's not easy to spot a team 20 points and come back, though. Not a team like the 49ers. They're good."

The turning point may have been the 49ers' goal-line stand in the third quarter. After the Bengals had closed to within 20–7, they drove to the 1-yard line but could not get the ball across on three tries.

The 1988 Super Bowl Season

A different coach—Sam Wyche—and a different quarterback—Boomer Esiason—led the Bengals to Super Bowl XXIII, their second Super Bowl in eight seasons. Unfortunately, they met the same team and the same fate—a loss to the San Francisco 49ers. But the ending didn't make the trip any less exciting. Here's a game-by-game look at the season.

September 4, in Cincinnati: Cincinnati 21, Phoenix 14. The Bengals used two big goal-line stands at the beginning of the game and the end to ruin the Cardinals' NFL debut. Phoenix took the opening kickoff and marched to a first down at the Bengals' 2-yard line, but failed to score. The Cardinals drove to the Bengals' 1-yard line late in the game, but two rushes lost yardage and one pass fell incomplete. Then, with a fourth-and-goal at the 9, Neil Lomax was sacked with eight seconds left.

September 11, at Philadelphia: Cincinnati 28, Philadelphia 24. Esiason and the Bengals emerged victorious after a quarterback shootout. Esiason completed 20 of 32 passes for 363 yards and four touchdowns. Randall Cunningham hit 25 of 36 passes for 261 yards

Coach Sam Wyche led the charge against the Buffalo Bills on January 8, 1989, as the Bengals won the AFC Championship 21–10 and earned a spot in Super Bowl XXIII.

and one touchdown, and he ran 85 yards on nine carries. "If you do what you're supposed to do, and do it right, you probably are going to have something happen," Esiason said.

September 18, at Pittsburgh: Cincinnati 17, Pittsburgh 12. Eddie Brown had only one catch, but it was an important one. His 65-yard touchdown reception early in the fourth quarter lifted the Bengals, who had to come back three times to win. Esiason completed 15 of 27 passes for 233 yards and two touchdowns.

September 25, in Cincinnati: Cincinnati 24, Cleveland 17. The Bengals ran past the Browns—literally. James Brooks had 17 carries for 83 yards, Stanley Wilson had 11 carries for 68 yards, and Ickey Woods had 13 carries for 62 yards and two touchdowns as the Bengals outgained the Browns on the ground, 213–68.

October 2, at Los Angeles: Cincinnati 45, Los Angeles Raiders 21. Esiason completed 21 of 28 passes for 332 yards and three touchdowns—and he only played three quarters. Esiason, leading the NFL in passing, completed 10 straight passes at one point as the Bengals improved to 5–0, becoming the only remaining unbeaten team in the league.

October 9, in Cincinnati: Cincinnati 36, New York Jets 19. The Jets jumped off to a 9–0 lead after a safety on the Bengals' first play and a fumble on their second. Somehow the Bengals managed to survive two missed extra points, a blocked field goal, a touchdown taken away by replay, and another fumble lost inside the 20. "We did a lot of things early that weren't too pretty," Wyche said. "Those things happen. Good teams overcome them, and I think we proved we're a good team."

October 16, at New England: New England 27, Cincinnati 21. It was bound to happen. Playing without Brooks, who was out with a fractured left hand, the Bengals weren't quite themselves and suffered their first loss of the 1988 season.

October 23, in Cincinnati: Cincinnati 44, Houston 21. Likely making up for the previous week, the Bengals jumped all over the

Oilers. Cincinnati took advantage of two turnovers and led 14–0 before Houston ran a play, 21–0 before Houston got a first down, and 28–0 before Houston completed a pass.

October 30, at Cleveland: Cleveland 23, Cincinnati 16. Herman Fontenot had a special day for the Browns, with an 84-yard kickoff return that set up Cleveland's first touchdown and a blocked punt return for another touchdown. Neither Esiason nor Browns quarterback Bernie Kosar threw a touchdown pass. Instead, the Browns defense came up big on three goal-line stands to stop the Bengals.

November 6, in Cincinnati: Cincinnati 42, Pittsburgh 7. Once again, the Bengals bounced back after a loss. Esiason completed 16 of 23 passes for 318 yards and three touchdowns. Brown had seven catches for a then single-game-record 216 yards. Brooks had three touchdowns. Pittsburgh coach Chuck Noll called it "the worst exhibition of football I've seen in a long time, from our viewpoint."

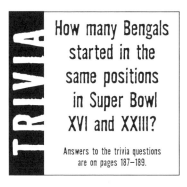

TRIVIA

How many Bengals started in the same positions in Super Bowl XVI and XXIII?

Answers to the trivia questions are on pages 187–189.

November 13, at Kansas City: Kansas City 31, Cincinnati 28. The Chiefs scored 12 points in the last 6:06 to stage the biggest upset of the season. They came into the game with the worst record in the NFL, while the Bengals had the highest-scoring offense. The rally started when the Chiefs blocked a punt for a safety. Then a pass interference call against David Fulcher set up a touchdown by Christian Okoye. Marc Logan fumbled the kickoff, which set up a game-winning 39-yard field goal by Nick Lowery with two seconds left. It was Lowery's fifth field goal of the game. Even Kansas City coach Frank Gansz seemed stunned by the turn of events. "We played probably one of the best football teams…in the history of the game," he said afterward.

Bengals Starting Lineups in Super Bowl XXIII

Offense		Defense	
WR	Tim McGee	LE	Jim Skow
LT	Anthony Muñoz	NT	Tim Krumrie
LG	Bruce Reimers	RE	Jason Buck
C	Bruce Kozerski	LOLB	Leon White
RG	Max Montoya	LILB	Carl Zander
RT	Brian Blados	RILB	Joe Kelly
TE	Rodney Holman	ROLB	Reggie Williams
WR	Eddie Brown	LCB	Lewis Billups
QB	Boomer Esiason	RCB	Eric Thomas
RB	James Brooks	SS	David Fulcher
FB	Ickey Woods	FS	Solomon Wilcots

November 20, at Dallas: Cincinnati 38, Dallas 24. The Bengals got back on track again as Esiason hit 20 of 36 passes for three touchdowns to hand Dallas its eighth straight loss. The Cowboys were suffering through their worst season since 1960.

November 27, in Cincinnati: Cincinnati 35, Buffalo 21. It was billed as Cincinnati's offense against Buffalo's defense, in a clash between the two best teams in the AFC. Offense won. Esiason completed 18 of 25 passes for 238 yards, and the Bengals also rushed for 232 yards. The Bills had allowed an average of only 101 yards rushing per game coming in. "This is by far and away the best offense we have seen," said Bills coach Marv Levy.

December 4, in Cincinnati: Cincinnati 27, San Diego 10. Brown's 37 yards receiving gave him a total of 1,157 for the season, a record at the time. Woods rushed for two touchdowns, giving him 15 rushing touchdowns for the season, tying another single-season record of the time.

DID YOU KNOW...

The 49ers' victory in Super Bowl XXIII made San Francisco the first NFC team to win three Super Bowls?

December 11, at Houston: Houston 41, Cincinnati 6. The number one offense in the league was held to just 226 yards. Mike Rozier was the star for the Oilers, with 22 carries for 126 yards and three touchdowns.

December 17, in Cincinnati: Cincinnati 20, Washington 17, in overtime. Jim Breech kicked a 20-yard field goal at 7:01 in overtime to win it. The Bengals caught a break when Washington rookie Chip Lohmiller hit the right upright with what would have been the game-winning 29-yard field goal with seven seconds left in regulation.

December 31, in Cincinnati: Cincinnati 21, Seattle 13. Wilson scored the Bengals' first two touchdowns on three-yard runs, and Woods scored the third. The Bengals scored all their points in the first half and then relied on their defense to advance to the AFC Championship game.

January 8, in Cincinnati: Cincinnati 21, Buffalo 10. The Bengals broke open a close game with a fake punt in the third quarter that set up Woods's second touchdown. But the day really belonged to the Bengals defense, which forced three interceptions by Jim Kelly and sacked him three times. Buffalo failed to convert on third down 10 times.

January 22, Super Bowl XXIII in Miami: San Francisco 20, Cincinnati 16. The ending was almost as painful as the beginning for the Bengals. Starting nose tackle Tim Krumrie suffered a gruesome broken leg early in the first quarter. But the Bengals, also playing without fullback Stanley Wilson (who had been suspended for a substance abuse violation the night before the game), persevered. The game was tied at halftime, 3–3, and it was just 6–6 late in the third quarter. Cincinnati's Stanford Jennings scored on a 93-yard kickoff return with 34 seconds left in the third quarter, but San Francisco answered with a 14-yard touchdown pass from Joe Montana to Jerry Rice just 1:31 later. Jim Breech kicked a 40-yard field goal, his third of the day, to put Cincinnati ahead, 16–13, with 3:20 remaining. But that was too much time for Montana. He led the 49ers on a 92-yard, 11-play drive capped by a 10-yard touchdown pass to John Taylor with 34 seconds left. Jerry Rice tied a Super Bowl record for receptions (originally set by Cincinnati's Dan Ross in Super Bowl XVI) with 11 receptions for 215 yards and a touchdown to win the MVP award. Montana was 23 of 36 for 357 yards and two touchdowns. Esiason was 11 of 25 for 144 yards with no touchdowns and one interception.

After the slow start, the game turned into a classic. Said NFL commissioner Pete Rozelle after the game, "Eddie DeBartolo, Coach Bill Walsh, you and the great Cincinnati team gave us the finest of our 23 Super Bowls. I don't think there is any question about that."

Chapter Seven

Notable Bengals

Chad Johnson: Talking a Good Game

It was a cold and rainy day in Cleveland. The Browns had played terribly in losing their opening game of the 2006 season, and the mood was as dark as the weather. Coach Romeo Crennel spoke in the press room, and then the reporters scattered to the adjacent locker room to see what the players had to say about the upcoming game at Cincinnati.

About noon, the door to the press room burst open, and the reporters started streaming back in. All of a sudden there was an electricity in the air, and the atmosphere seemed lighter.

Had the Browns players been that entertaining? Had an assistant coach offered a ray of hope?

No, no. The change had nothing whatsoever to do with the Browns. Rather, the reporters were expecting a call from Chad Johnson, the Bengals' outspoken wide receiver.

Every week during the National Football League season, usually on Wednesdays, the upcoming opponents hold a conference call with

141

Never the wallflower, wide receiver Chad Johnson happily struts his stuff whenever the opportunity knocks.

the media. In general, the opposing coach speaks first, followed by a player selected by the media.

Johnson is a perennial favorite, and the main reason why the reporters hustled back to the press room on this otherwise gloomy day. Whereas too many coaches and players talk about "what a fine football team" they're facing or "taking one game at a time," no one ever knows what Johnson will say. Or do, for that matter.

This is, after all, the guy who once sent bottles of Pepto-Bismol to the Browns defensive backs the week before they had to cover him. This is the guy who once performed CPR on the football after scoring a touchdown. On this day, it took Johnson a little while to warm up. But in the end, he did not disappoint.

Actually, he was responsible for the whole exchange. Reporters followed up on comments Johnson made in the summer of 2006 about Browns cornerback Leigh Bodden. Johnson, who led the American Football Conference in receiving yards for the third straight year in 2005, told a national radio audience that Bodden was the only player who covered him during the 2005 season. In the second game between the Bengals and the Browns that season, Johnson, covered by Bodden, had just two catches for 22 yards.

Unlike his comments on the national radio show, Johnson didn't seem to want to give Bodden much credit this time around, insisting that he and quarterback Carson Palmer were just off on their timing that day. But the more questions the reporters asked, the more agitated Johnson became.

Finally came the outburst they'd been waiting for.

"Have you ever seen anyone cover me before?" Johnson asked one reporter. "I have six years' worth of film. Go get all of them and find one [defensive back] that's stopped me. Did you see anyone physically stop me? You saw me drop balls, the Pepto game, right? And last year, the second game here, you saw balls drop all over the place because it was a heavy-wind game. You didn't see anyone knock the ball down, physically jam mc at the line, re-route me, any of that stuff.

"C'mon now. Let's talk football. Stop thinking like a writer for a minute and talk football. It's humanly impossible to stop [number] 85. I'm trying to talk your kind of talk, but now you're kind of…I don't even know the word to use…insulting me a little bit. I cannot be stopped, period. I gave the guy his credit because we were off as a team, but you're taking it overboard."

Get the idea? Johnson loves to talk, and reporters love to listen to him. This is a man who titled his authorized biography *Chad: I Can't Be Stopped* by Paul Daugherty. He's talking about his play, but he could just as easily be talking about his gift for gab.

What's important for the Bengals is that he usually backs up his words on the field. In 2005, he set a Bengals record with 1,432 yards receiving and a career-high 97 catches. Those statistics earned him his third straight start in the Pro Bowl and his first nod as a first-team All-Pro. In 2006, he had another Pro Bowl year, with 87 catches for an NFL-leading 1,369 yards and seven touchdowns. He became the first Bengals player to lead the league in receiving yards and the first player to lead his conference in receiving yards for the fourth straight time.

TRIVIA

Chad Johnson has two cousins who are NFL players. Can you name them?

Answers to the trivia questions are on pages 187–189.

He gained even more yards in 2007 (1,440) on 93 receptions, finishing second to Reggie Wayne of Indianapolis.

Those were the sort of numbers the Bengals hoped for when they made Johnson a second-round draft choice (the 36th player taken overall) in 2001 after his junior year at Oregon State. In his one season with the team, he averaged 21.8 yards per reception to help Oregon State to a number four ranking and a Fiesta Bowl victory over Notre Dame.

Thousand-Yard Duos

There have been ten seasons in which the Bengals have had both a 1,000-yard rusher and a 1,000-yard receiver, according to the team's press guide. (Rushers are listed first.)

1981: Pete Johnson (1,077) and Cris Collinsworth (1,009)
1986: James Brooks (1,087) and Cris Collinsworth (1,024)
1988: Ickey Woods (1,066) and Eddie Brown (1,273)
1989: James Brooks (1,239) and Tim McGee (1,211)
1998: Corey Dillon (1,130) and Carl Pickens (1,023)
1999: Corey Dillon (1,200) and Darnay Scott (1,022)
2002: Corey Dillon (1,311) and Chad Johnson (1,166)
2004: Rudi Johnson (1,454) and Chad Johnson (1,274)
2005: Rudi Johnson (1,458) and Chad Johnson (1,432)
2006: Rudi Johnson (1,309) and Chad Johnson (1,369), T.J. Houshmandzadeh (1,081)

How he got to Corvallis is a story in itself.

Johnson, born January 9, 1978, grew up in the Liberty City area of Miami. He and his mother, Paula Johnson, lived with her mother, Bessie Mae Flowers, and stepfather, James Flowers. When Chad Johnson was five years old, his mother took his little brother Chauncey and moved to Los Angeles, leaving Chad in the care of his grandmother, a taskmaster who had taught English and reading to students in Miami's public schools. Paula Johnson wanted her son to have the same sort of upbringing she'd had, and she thought it was best to leave Chad in the care of his grandmother. She talked to her son nearly every night, and he spent summer vacations with her in Los Angeles. But it was Bessie Mae Flowers who raised Johnson.

She tried to keep her grandson from the burgeoning trouble in the streets of their neighborhood, driving him to school and football practices up to 45 minutes away in places like Miami Beach and

DID YOU KNOW...

That Chad Johnson is a fan of musicals like *West Side Story* and that he still occasionally sucks his thumb? Those facts were revealed in *Chad: I Can't Be Stopped*, by Paul Daugherty, published by Orange Frazer Press in Wilmington, Ohio, in 2006.

Coral Gables. Johnson, who started playing football when he was four, played wide receiver for three years at Miami Beach High School and, as the team's best athlete, was switched to quarterback as a senior.

Unfortunately, Chad Johnson wasn't much of a student. He wasn't really a troublemaker, he just didn't like to go to class. In fact, he skipped so many classes that he needed to go to summer school in order to graduate and be eligible to play football at a junior college.

He started out at Langston University in Oklahoma in 1996 but was expelled for fighting. His grandmother wouldn't let him come back home after that, so he moved in with his mother and attended Santa Monica College in California. His penchant for cutting class kicked in again, so it took him three years to complete a two-year program and he had to sit out the 1998 football season to get his grades in order. But in the two years he was eligible, he played 20 games and caught 120 passes for 2,100 yards and 23 touchdowns.

That caught the attention of Oregon State coach Dennis Erickson, who managed to convince Johnson to make the move north and stay eligible for one spectacular year, a year that enabled him to make the National Football League.

Johnson became an instant hit in Cincinnati because, despite a decade of futility, he maintained that he wanted to play there.

"I didn't want to go somewhere they were already winning," he said in his book, *Chad: I Can't Be Stopped*. "I wanted to be the reason we started winning. I had no problems being a Cincinnati Bengal."

Seven years later, Johnson is one of the most popular athletes in town, and undoubtedly the most vocal. Oddly enough, given his academic history, he has also become a student of the game, studying hours upon hours of game films of his opponents. More than once, he has fallen asleep at the team's facility while watching films, prompting the Bengals to provide him with DVDs he can take home and watch. In his quest to become the best wide receiver in the history of the game, he and quarterback Carson Palmer drove from Cincinnati to Indianapolis to watch Colts quarterback Peyton Manning and wide receiver Marvin Harrison in one Monday night game. Those two are considered the best in the game these days.

Johnson also appreciates the history of the game. Before a game against visiting Green Bay in 2005, Johnson asked Packers quarterback Brett Favre, a shoo-in for the Hall of Fame, to throw him a pass, just so he could say he'd caught one. Of course, if Johnson has his way, someday Favre may be bragging about throwing a pass to Johnson.

Johnson's outspoken nature has gotten him into trouble on occasion. The NFL has fined him numerous times for his touchdown celebrations, which have ranged from proposing to a cheerleader to putting with a pylon. He also has no problem telling his teammates and coaches he needs to be involved more; he even asked to be traded after the 2007 season. By and large, the Bengals have gotten used to that, chalking it up to Johnson's competitive nature, and it doesn't cause the problems it might elsewhere.

NFL Quarterback and Regular Guy

Carson Palmer's blog on his official website, www.carsonpalmer9.com, has an interesting subtitle: "The Latest on My Life as an NFL Quarterback and Regular Guy." The question is, can an NFL starting quarterback on one of the best teams in the league, a Heisman Trophy winner at USC, and the number one overall pick in the 2003 draft really be a regular guy?

From the looks of his website, it's entirely possible.

He lists his favorite food as pizza, his favorite television show as *Family Guy,* and his favorite pro athlete as LeBron James. Golf is his favorite sport and his favorite hobby; a golf club is his favorite toy; and if he had to be something other than an NFL quarterback, he says his dream job would be pro golfer. He likes country music, has dogs named Homer and Muffin, and says Homer is his best friend.

So far he sounds like about 90 percent of the guys in the cubicles next to yours.

Okay, so maybe the guy next to you can't say winning the Orange Bowl was his biggest achievement or winning the Super Bowl is his biggest goal—and have a legitimate chance to actually accomplish

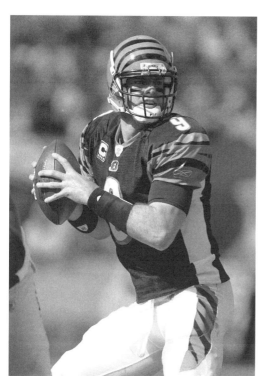

Despite his career as a record-holding quarterback and Pro Bowler, Carson Palmer claims he's just a regular guy.

that. But otherwise, the Big Kahuna (that's Palmer's nickname) really sounds just like any other guy.

His blog is full of chatty references to everyday events, like grocery shopping at Meijer and shooting an 85 on the golf course. It was Torrey Pines, but hey, that could happen to anyone. He asks fans to continue posting, and he refers to several who have by name. He also talks about a trip to watch his little brother, Jordan, play quarterback at University of Texas at El Paso (UTEP), where he insists he's referred to as Jordan Palmer's older brother.

TRIVIA

Carson Palmer was the second true freshman to start at quarterback for Southern Cal; who was the first?

Answers to the trivia questions are on pages 187–189.

But when Palmer steps onto the football field, it's clear he is not a regular guy. In 2006, he completed 324 of 520 passes for a team-record 4,035 yards, 28 touchdowns, and a quarterback rating of 93.9—a season that earned him a trip to the Pro Bowl. In 2007, it was a team-record 4,131 yards with a team-record 373 completions.

That Palmer was ready to start the 2006 season surprised many who saw the severe knee injury he suffered in the Bengals' wild-card playoff loss to the Pittsburgh Steelers on January 8, 2006. On the Bengals' second offensive play, Pittsburgh's Kimo von Oelhoffen hit Palmer after the quarterback completed a 66-yard pass to Chris Henry. Palmer suffered a torn ACL and MCL in his left knee, dislocated his kneecap, and injured cartilage and tissue as well. Although he maintained the hit was a clean one, Palmer cried when he got the diagnosis in the training room. It was a devastating end to the Bengals' breakthrough season, and at least temporarily caused concerns that maybe the team was not going to turn things around after all.

Dr. Lonnie F. Paulos performed surgery in Houston two days after the injury, and two days after that Palmer returned to his home in southern California to begin rehabilitation. In his blog, he told fans, "This is going to be a long, grueling process but knowing that you all will be waiting for me at the Jungle provides me with great inspiration."

The intensity Palmer brought to his rehabilitation was inspiring to his teammates.

"He worked three times harder than the normal person is supposed to work when you have that type of injury," wide receiver Chad Johnson said before the Bengals faced the Browns early in the 2006 season. "He worked crazy hard throughout the entire off-season."

How important did the outspoken receiver think Palmer's return was?

"He gives us our best chance to win the Super Bowl," Johnson said. "It's as easy as that. I think Carson is probably the best quarterback in the game. The only thing other quarterbacks might have on him is a little more experience because they've been playing the game longer."

Longer, maybe, but not many have achieved the success Palmer has in his young career.

Carson grew up in Mission Viejo, California, and attended Santa Margarita High School, where he set 27 school records. As a senior in 1997, he threw 31 touchdowns and just four interceptions to lead the school to a 14–0 record and its second straight state title. He was such a dedicated athlete that the day after winning the state title in football, he was right on time for a 10:00 AM basketball practice the next morning.

DID YOU KNOW...

That Palmer became the second Bengals player to have won the Heisman Trophy? Running back Archie Griffin, the only back-to-back winner, who received the honor in 1974 and 1975 at Ohio State, was the first.

At Southern Cal, he started four games his freshman year, becoming just the second true freshman to start at quarterback in the illustrious history of the program. His sophomore year was cut short by a broken collarbone in the third game, but the good news was that he redshirted that year so as not to lose a season of eligibility. The extra year paid off; by the time he was a senior, he and the Trojans were almost unstoppable.

In 2002, Palmer led the Trojans to eight straight victories at the end of the season as USC, with an 11–2 record, beat Iowa in the Orange Bowl, 38–17. He set Pacific-10 conference records in passing yards, with 11,818; completions, with 927; and total offense, with 11,621. His 72 career touchdown passes set a USC record. As a senior, he also set single-season records for completions, with 309; passing yards, with 3,942; and touchdown passes, with 33. It is no wonder he won the Heisman Trophy.

Though the Bengals made him the first pick overall in the draft, he did not play in a regular-season game as a rookie; the team opted to bring him along slowly behind Jon Kitna. Once new coach Marvin Lewis came on board in 2004, Palmer was the starter, at least until a strained knee ligament in Game 13 ended his season prematurely. The Bengals were 8–8 that season, ending a string of six straight seasons below .500. Palmer completed 263 of 432 passes for 2,897 yards and 18 touchdowns.

As the Bengals improved to 11–5 in 2005, Palmer improved, too. He completed 345 of 509 passes for 3,836 yards and 32 touchdowns. His quarterback rating was 101.1.

The injury threatened all that—or at least that was what people who didn't know Palmer thought. His resolve to come back never wavered.

"I'm amazed, really," Pittsburgh coach Bill Cowher said before the Bengals faced the Steelers for the first time in 2006. "Number one, just watching him go through it, listening to him this whole off-season, just the determination he had to be back out there. The positives and the sacrifices that he made to get there, it's a true credit to Carson. He's good for the league."

The Quiet Johnson

Rudi Johnson is the quiet one—at least when compared to teammate Chad Johnson.

Whereas wide receiver Chad Johnson never met an interviewer he didn't like, has published a book about himself, and plans his end-zone celebrations after touchdowns, running back Rudi Johnson tends to let his play speak for him. Since becoming the Bengals' featured back in the 2004 season, that play has screamed success—especially against the Cleveland Browns.

Starting when Rudi Johnson gained a career-high 202 yards in a 58–48 victory over the visiting Browns on November 28, 2004, the Bengals won five straight against the Browns, and Johnson averaged 27 carries and 141.2 yards in each of those victories.

After running for 169 yards in a 23–20 Bengals victory on December 11, 2005, Johnson was asked why he was so successful against Cleveland.

"I don't know," he told reporters. "Whatever it is, I'll take it. Don't change it. I guess it's just knowing their personnel. Who knows? Whatever it is, I'll take it, year in and year out."

Rudi Johnson is the latest in the Bengals' long line of strong running backs, following the likes of Pete Johnson, James Brooks, Ickey Woods, and Corey Dillon. In order to make sure that line continued uninterrupted, the Bengals signed Rudi Johnson to a five-year, $26 million deal on March 16, 2005.

Chad Johnson applauded the move.

"You can't really appreciate a back like Rudi until you play with him," Chad Johnson told reporters. "Rudi has size and speed, the combination of everything. Most backs have one thing. But Rudi can do it all—bounce it outside and run up in between the tackles. He's a complete back."

It's the threat of Rudi Johnson that keeps defenses honest when it comes to coverage on Chad Johnson.

"You pick your poison when you put your coverage to Chad or Rudi," Cleveland coach Romeo Crennel said before Cincinnati's 30–0 victory in Cleveland on November 26, 2006. "Chad can put up big numbers himself, but if you worry too much about Chad, Rudi will be running the ball on you."

Rudi Johnson hardly exploded onto the scene in Cincinnati. He was a fourth-round draft choice out of Auburn, the 100th player taken overall. He barely played as a rookie, and never as a running back. Instead, the Bengals used him on special teams, where he had four kickoff returns for 79 yards.

Running back Rudi Johnson is known as the "quiet one" because he lets his plays speak for themselves. In 2005, the sure-handed Rudi Johnson was a major reason the Bengals led the league in fewest lost fumbles—six, a team record.

DID YOU KNOW...

That Johnson is the most common last name on the Bengals' all-time roster? There have been 18 players named Johnson who played for Cincinnati. The last name Smith is second, with 14, and Williams is third, with 13.

Things didn't get appreciably better his second season. He had 17 carries for 67 yards rushing, six receptions for 34 yards receiving, and 13 kickoff returns for 277 yards. He was inactive for nine of the Bengals' 16 games.

Johnson was inactive for the first three games of the 2003 season with a strained quadriceps, but then fate intervened. Starter Corey Dillon injured his groin, and the Bengals called Johnson's number— again and again. He was so productive that even when Dillon returned, the two split time, and it was Johnson who ended up as the Bengals' leading rusher that season, with 215 carries for 957 yards and nine touchdowns. He gained 100 yards for the first time on October 26 against Seattle, when he had 101, and followed that with 182 yards against Houston and 165 against Kansas City in back-to-back games on November 9 and November 16, respectively. He also had 174 yards against San Francisco on December 14, becoming the only Bengals player to run for more than 150 yards in three games in one season.

His emergence that season allowed the Bengals to trade the disgruntled Dillon to New England and move Johnson into the starting lineup permanently. In his first season as a starter, he set team records for carries (with 361) and rushing yards (with 1,454) and earned a trip to the Pro Bowl as an injury replacement for the Jets' Curtis Martin. In the Pro Bowl, Johnson led the AFC with 33 yards on six carries.

The 2005 season was even better. Johnson, a Pro Bowl alternate, broke the team rushing record again with 1,458 yards, which ranked him fourth in the AFC and seventh in the NFL. He had just one fumble in 360 touches, which helped the Bengals lead the NFL with a team-record-low number of fumbles lost—six. He ranked third in the AFC with 337 carries and tied for sixth in the AFC with 12 touchdowns, one of which came in that monster game against the Browns.

"It's fun sitting back there behind him when he's going like that," Bengals quarterback Carson Palmer said of Johnson after that game. "He kept shaking and he kept moving. It makes it a lot easier on an offense."

In 2006, Johnson rushed 341 times for 1,309 yards and 12 touchdowns. In 2007, he rushed 170 times for 497 yards.

Johnson, 5'10" and 228 pounds, was born October 1, 1979, in Ettrick, Virginia. His father, Melvin, was a security guard. His mother, Janice, sold insurance. He has three brothers and two sisters. He attended Thomas Dale High School in Chester, Virginia, before enrolling at Butler County Community College in El Dorado, Kansas. In 1999, he rushed for 2,224 yards and 35 touchdowns. In the junior college championship game, he rushed for 373 yards and seven touchdowns in Butler's 49–35 victory over Dixie College, and was an easy choice for the Most Valuable Player award.

TRIVIA

What is Rudi Johnson's full name?

Answers to the trivia questions are on pages 187–189.

He played only one season at Auburn, but it was a memorable one, and he was named the coaches' Player of the Year in the Southeastern Conference. He was the Associated Press SEC Offensive Player of the Year and was a semifinalist for the Doak Walker Award, given to the nation's top running back. He set a school single-season rushing record with 324 carries, and his 1,567 rushing yards were the second most in school history, trailing only Bo Jackson's 1,786 in 1985. He rushed for 100 or more yards in 10 games, and he had touchdown runs of 78, 70, 56, and 42 yards.

Riding the Waves

It's not the sort of thing they keep statistics on, not the kind of trend anyone tracks.

But have you ever noticed how many former Bengals become broadcasters? You can hardly turn on the radio or television these days without coming across someone who played in Cincinnati.

In fact, when the Bengals played host to the Baltimore Ravens on November 30, 2006, in a game broadcast on the NFL Network, it was more like Old Home Week. No fewer than seven former Bengals were at the game in some broadcasting capacity, including Cris Collinsworth as the NFL Network analyst; Sam Wyche on Westwood One Radio; and Dave Lapham, David Fulcher, and Eric Thomas as members of the local media corps. It was hard to tell if it was a game or a reunion.

In an article on Bengals.com, website editor Geoff Hobson's column carried the headline "PBC airs from PBS." The translation? Paul Brown Channel airs from Paul Brown Stadium.

Though his impact on the franchise is inescapable and far-reaching, Brown could never have known that he was grooming an entire generation of players who would take their knowledge from the football field to the airwaves.

"I happen to think that the number of former Bengals who went on to work as football broadcasters was greatly influenced by the organization's heritage of outstanding coaching, all of which began with Paul Brown," said Tom Merritt, the former head of public relations at NBC. "Brown was a believer in a total team environment where his players knew what was going on with the

DID YOU KNOW...

That Solomon Wilcots appears with Adam Schein and Jim Miller on *The Afternoon Blitz* on Sirius NFL Radio?

team on both sides of the ball. In evaluating and acquiring players, Brown liked kids with smarts who would be good students of his teaching.

"Brown had many outstanding assistants who learned from and carried on his manner of teaching when they became head coaches. Certainly, many of the Bengals who went into broadcasting were influenced by Bill Walsh, who was with Brown from the beginning of the franchise until Brown retired from the sidelines in 1975. We all know what Walsh achieved in San Francisco, where he became known as the master of the West Coast offense, but I have to believe that Walsh's offensive philosophy and strategy rubbed off on Bengals players—sort of like a head-start course for those who had a future in broadcasting in mind."

Dave Lapham agrees completely.

"In my opinion, the common denominator is Paul," said Lapham, the former offensive lineman who just completed his 22nd consecutive season as the analyst on Bengals radio broadcasts. "I think Paul was a very innovative thinker. As a result of that, he made football intriguing. He wanted you to look beyond what you were doing and see the big picture—what you were doing and why it was that way, based on what everybody else around you was doing. He was always looking for a way to advance the game.

"I had Bill Walsh as a passing game coordinator. Bill was a master innovator. Dick LeBeau was very innovative with the defense and his zone blitz. Sam Wyche was the ultimate innovative guy with his no-huddle offense.

"Paul basically piqued your interest. He was such a great teacher of the game. He was my inspiration. Part of it is that everybody who's involved in broadcasting was exposed to the Super Bowl phenomenon. You're involved with the media there. I was intrigued by the media days. I thought, 'That's not a bad job,' because you were still very much in touch with the game. I think the Super Bowl exposure was part of it for me, too."

A pack of striped helmets is all that can be seen in this celebratory pile-on after a game-winning catch by Chad Johnson, in 2004.

Lapham played two seasons for Brown, who retired as coach after the 1975 season. When Solomon Wilcots arrived as a defensive back in 1987, Brown was the general manager who had hired Wyche as coach, so his influence continued.

"We were cutting-edge in terms of our coach in Sam Wyche, who had helped Bill Walsh as an assistant," said Wilcots, who has worked in a variety of positions on the local and national broadcasting scene. "Bill Walsh was the offensive coordinator under Paul Brown for years and started the West Coast offense in Cincinnati. We had that kind of offense. We had a zone-blocking scheme with offensive line coach Jim McNally, which was a cutting-edge thing with Anthony Muñoz and Max Montoya. We had a prolific quarterback in Boomer Esiason, a great leader. We had a cutting-edge defense in the zone blitz scheme that no one else knew about.

"I learned from some great coaches. We had some intelligent guys in our locker room. We had great locker-room lawyers who could debate the finer points of life—politics and football. We had a coach who compelled us to be thinkers. Because we had coaches like that— Jim McNally on the offensive line, [offensive coordinator] Bruce Coslet was a creative guy, Sam Wyche was very innovative, [defensive coordinator] Dick LeBeau…when you have a collection of individuals who are learning from those kinds of coaches, and they're all very outspoken, you're going to spawn some guys who are going to go out and do some things in life."

Wilcots noted that Collinsworth was a natural, as was Esiason.

"I don't know that they'd tell you they saw it from me, because I was the kind of guy who only talked in games," Wilcots said, laughing. "I was a young player. I didn't have the right to talk. I just had to play. But Dick LeBeau groomed me to be a safety. Cornerbacks just kind of go out and cover their guys. Safeties have to be more vocal. So it was at that point that I started to be a more vocal guy."

Bengals Who Could Have a Future in Broadcasting

1. Chad Johnson
2. Carson Palmer
3. T.J. Houshmandzadeh

Wilcots started his broadcasting career as an intern for the NBC affiliate in Cincinnati. Gradually, his resume grew to include producer, editor, weekend sports anchor, and radio show host. He left Cincinnati in 1998 to become a bureau correspondent for ESPN, and later joined CBS. During the 2007 season, in addition to CBS, he worked for the NFL Network as a studio analyst and feature reporter, did NFL radio for Sirius, and wrote columns for NFL.com, putting his degree in English literature from the University of Colorado to good use.

He and his family are back in Cincinnati, a city he credits for his success and that of the former players who have joined him in the broadcasting business.

"Everyone here is proud of us," he said. "It's a wonderful place to live. It's the kind of town where if you buy into the community, if you invest in the community, they'll love you. It's a small enough market where you're allowed to get on television and radio and make your mistakes early on. They'll forgive you. It's not a scrutinizing group. They'll say, 'Oh, that's just Solomon. It's okay.' You're able to get your at-bats until you get pretty good at it. In that sense, Cincinnati has been good to all of us because it allowed to cut our teeth, if you will, in broadcasting…if you were playing in New York or Chicago and you weren't coming out of the blocks smoking and as smooth as Tiki Barber, it wouldn't work."

Because of the variety of jobs he has held, Wilcots is often asked for advice by students or athletes interested in broadcasting. First, he tells them the importance of reading and writing as preparation. "Reading is like making a deposit, and writing is like making a withdrawal," he said.

Then he tells them they're lucky to be living in Cincinnati.

"When I talk to young groups and go to colleges and universities to talk to kids about broadcasting, I try to get them to understand that being a broadcaster is like being a lawyer," he said. "There are various disciplines. Just because you're a good divorce lawyer doesn't mean you're good at mergers and acquisitions. Just because you're a good business lawyer doesn't mean you're a good defense lawyer. So, just because you're a good radio host doesn't mean you're a good game analyst. Just because you're a good studio host doesn't mean you can call games as a play-by-play guy. [Being] a sideline reporter requires a whole other kind of technique. [Being] a feature reporter is vastly different.

"I work with a lot of former players and try to get them to understand: make sure you know what you're doing because you don't want to get out there and drop the ball. You've got to find a place to get your reps in all these areas before you go prime-time. You want to make sure you're a polished product. But it's difficult to get experience in all levels. You've got to start somewhere."

Appendix

All-Time Roster

Player	College	Years with Bengals
Abdullah, Khalid (LB)	Mars Hill	2003–04
Adams, Blue (CB)	Cincinnati	2007
Adams, Doug (LB)	Ohio State	1971–74
Adams, Sam (DT)	Texas A&M	2006
Alexander, Charles (RB)	Louisiana State	1979–85
Alexis, Alton (WR)	Tulane	1980
Ambrose, Ashley (CB)	Mississippi Valley State	1996–98
Amsler, Martin (DE)	Evansville	1970
Anderson, Jerry (S)	Oklahoma	1977
Anderson, Ken (QB)	Augustana (Illinois)	1971–86
Anderson, Willie (T)	Auburn	1996–07
Andrews, Stacy (T)	Mississippi	2004–07
Archer, Dan (T)	Oregon	1968
Armour, JoJuan (S)	Miami (Ohio)	1999–2002
Aronson, Doug (G)	San Diego State	1987
Arthur, Mike (C)	Texas A&M	1991–92

Askew, Matthias (DT)	Michigan State	2004–05
Avery, Ken (LB)	Southern Mississippi	1969–74
Baccaglio, Martin (DE)	San Jose State	1968–70
Bacon, Coy (DE)	Jackson State	1976–77
Bahr, Chris (K)	Penn State	1976–79
Bailey, Thomas (WR)	Auburn	1995
Ball, Eric (RB)	UCLA	1989–94
Banks, Estes (RB)	Colorado	1968
Bankston, Michael (DE)	Sam Houston State	1998–2000
Barber, Chris (S)	North Carolina A&T	1987–89
Barber, Mike (WR)	Marshall	1990–92
Barker, Leo (LB)	New Mexico State	1984–91
Barndt, Tom (DT)	Pittsburgh	2000
Basnight, Michael (RB)	North Carolina A&T	1999–2000
Bass, Don (WR)	Houston	1978–81
Battaglia, Marco (TE)	Rutgers	1996–2001
Battle, Ralph (DB)	Jacksonville State	1984
Bauman, Rashad (CB)	Oregon	2004–06
Bean, Robert (CB)	Mississippi State	2000–01
Beauchamp, Al (LB)	Southern U.	1968–75
Beckett, Rogers (S)	Marshall	2003–04
Bell, Leonard (S)	Indiana	1987
Bell, Myron (S)	Michigan State	1998–99
Benjamin, Ryan (RB)	Pacific	1993
Bennett, Antoine (CB)	Florida A&M	1991–92
Bennett, Ben (QB)	Duke	1987
Bennett, Brandon (RB)	South Carolina	1998–2003
Bentley, Ray (LB)	Central Michigan	1992
Bergey, Bill (LB)	Arkansas State	1969–73
Berry, Royce (DE)	Houston	1969–75
Berthusen, Bill (DE)	Iowa State	1987
Bieniemy, Eric (RB)	Colorado	1995–98
Billups, Lewis (CB)	North Alabama	1986–91
Blackman, Ken (G)	Illinois	1996–99

Blackmon, Roosevelt (CB)	Morris Brown	1998–99
Blackwood, Lyle (S)	TCU	1973–75
Blados, Brian (G)	North Carolina	1984–91
Blair, Michael (RB)	Ball State	1998
Blake, Jeff (QB)	East Carolina	1994–99
Body, Patrick (CB)	Toledo	2005
Booker, Vaughn (DE)	Cincinnati	2000–02
Borders, Nate (S)	Indiana	1987
Boyarsky, Jerry (NT)	Pittsburgh	1982–85
Boyd, LaVell (WR)	Louisville	2000
Brabham, Dan (LB)	Arkansas	1968
Bradley, Chuck (T)	Kentucky	1993
Brady, Ed (LB)	Illinois	1986–91
Braham, Rich (C)	West Virginia	1994–2006
Bramlet, Casey (QB)	Wyoming	2004
Braxton, David (LB)	Wake Forest	1994
Brazell, Bennie (WR)	Louisiana State	2006
Breech, Jim (K)	California	1980–92
Breeden, Louis (CB)	N. Carolina Central	1978–87
Breen, Adrian (QB)	Morehead State	1987
Brennan, Brian (WR)	Boston College	1992
Brennan, Mike (T)	Notre Dame	1990–91
Brewer, Sean (TE)	San Jose State	2001–02
Brice, Will (P)	Virginia	1999
Bright, Greg (S)	Morehead State	1980–81
Brilz, Darrick (C)	Oregon State	1994–98
Brim, Mike (CB)	Virginia Union	1993–95
Brooks, Ahmad (LB)	Virginia	2006-07
Brooks, Billy (WR)	Oklahoma	1976–79
Brooks, Greg (CB)	Southern Mississippi	2004–06
Brooks, James (RB)	Auburn	1984–91
Broussard, Steve (RB)	Washington State	1994
Brown, Anthony (T)	Utah	1995–98
Brown, Bob (DT)	Arkansas A,M&N	1975–76
Brown, Eddie (WR)	Miami (Florida)	1985–91

Brown, Ken (WR)	Southern Arkansas	1987
Brown, Tom (WR)	Augustana (South Dakota)	1987
Browner, Jim (S)	Notre Dame	1979–80
Browner, Ross (DE)	Notre Dame	1978–86
Brumfield, Scott (G)	Brigham Young	1993–97
Buchanan, Tim (LB)	Hawaii	1969
Buck, Jason (DE)	Brigham Young	1987–90
Buckner, Brentson (NT)	Clemson	1997
Buie, Drew (WR)	Catawba	1972
Bujnoch, Glenn (G)	Texas A&M	1976–82
Buncom, Frank (LB)	Southern California	1968
Burk, Scott (S)	Oklahoma State	1979
Burley, Gary (DE)	Pittsburgh	1975–83
Burns, Jason (RB)	Wisconsin	1995
Burris, Jeff (CB)	Notre Dame	2002–03
Bush, Blair (C)	Washington	1978–82
Bush, Steve (TE)	Arizona State	1997–2000
Busing, John (S)	Miami (Ohio)	2006-07
Bussey, Barney (S)	South Carolina State	1986–92
Cadigan, Dave (G)	Southern California	1994
Cameron, Glenn (LB)	Florida	1975–85
Canale, Justin (G)	Mississippi State	1969
Carey, Richard (CB)	Idaho	1989
Carpenter, Ron (DT)	North Carolina State	1970–76
Carpenter, Ron (S)	Miami (Ohio)	1993
Carroll, Wesley (WR)	Miami (Florida)	1993
Carter, Carl (CB)	Texas Tech	1990
Carter, Chris (S)	Texas	2000–01
Carter, Ki-Jana (RB)	Penn State	1995–99
Carter, Tom (CB)	Notre Dame	1999–2001
Carter, Virgil (QB)	Brigham Young	1970–73
Casanova, Tommy (S)	Louisiana State	1972–77
Catchings, Toney (LB)	Cincinnati	1987
Chamberlin, Frank (LB)	Boston College	2003–04

Chandler, Al (TE)	Oklahoma	1973–74
Chapman, Clarence (CB)	Eastern Michigan	1980–81
Chatman, Antonio (WR)	Cincinnati	2006–07
Chevrier, Randy (LS)	McGill (Canada)	2001
Chomyszak, Steve (DT)	Syracuse	1968–73
Christensen, Jeff (QB)	Eastern Illinois	1983
Clark, Bernard (LB)	Miami (Florida)	1990–91
Clark, Boobie (RB)	Bethune-Cookman	1973–78
Clark, Bryan (QB)	Michigan State	1984
Clark, Rico (CB)	Louisville	1999
Clark, Wayne (QB)	U.S. International	1974
Clemons, Duane (DE)	California	2003–05
Coats, Daniel (TE)	Brigham Young	2007
Coats, Tony (G)	Washington	1999
Cobb, Marvin (S)	Southern California	1975–79
Cobb, Mike (TE)	Michigan State	1977
Coleman, Al (S)	Tennessee State	1969–71
Coleman, Reggie (TE)	Tennessee	2002
Collins, Andre (LB)	Penn State	1995–97
Collins, Gerald (LB)	Vanderbilt	1995
Collins, Glen (DE)	Mississippi State	1982–85
Collinsworth, Cris (WR)	Florida	1981–88
Conley, Steve (RB)	Kansas	1972
Cook, Greg (QB)	Cincinnati	1969–74
Copeland, John (DE)	Alabama	1993–2000
Corbett, Jim (TE)	Pittsburgh	1977–80
Cornish, Frank (DT)	Grambling	1970
Coslet, Bruce (TE)	Pacific	1969–76
Costello, Brad (P)	Boston U.	1998–99
Cothran, Jeff (FB)	Ohio State	1994–96
Cotton, Barney (G)	Nebraska	1979
Cousino, Brad (LB)	Miami (Ohio)	1975
Covington, Scott (QB)	Miami (Florida)	1999–2001
Crabtree, Eric (WR)	Pittsburgh	1969–71
Craig, Neal (S)	Fisk	1971–73

Cupp, Keith (T)	Findlay	1987
Curtis, Canute (LB)	West Virginia	1997–2002
Curtis, Isaac (WR)	San Diego State	1973–84
Davidson, Kenny (DE)	Louisiana State	1996
Davis, Charlie (RB)	Colorado	1974–75
Davis, Lee (CB)	Mississippi	1985
Davis, Oliver (S)	Tennessee State	1981–82
Davis, Ricky (S)	Alabama	1975
Davis, Tony (RB)	Nebraska	1976–78
Dawson, Clifton (RB)	Harvard	2007
DeAyala, Kiki (LB)	Texas	1986–87
DeGraffenreid, Allen (WR)	Ohio State	1993
DeLeone, Tom (G)	Ohio State	1972
DeMarco, Brian (G)	Michigan State	1999
Dennis, Guy (G)	Florida	1969–72
Dennis, Mark (T)	Illinois	1994
DePaso, Tom (LB)	Penn State	1978
Devlin, Chris (LB)	Penn State	1975–78
Dillahunt, Ellis (S)	East Carolina	1988
Dillon, Corey (RB)	Washington	1997–2003
Dingle, Mike (RB)	South Carolina	1991–92
Dinkel, Tom (LB)	Kansas	1978–83, 1985
Dixon, Gerald (LB)	South Carolina	1996–97
Dixon, Rickey (CB)	Oklahoma	1988–92
Donahue, Mark (G)	Michigan	1978–79
Dorsch, Travis (P)	Purdue	2002
Dorsey, DeDe (RB)	Lindenwood	2007
Doughty, Mike (T)	Notre Dame	1999–2000
Douglas, David (T)	Tennessee	1986–88
Douthard, Ty (RB)	Illinois	1997
Dressler, Doug (RB)	Chico State	1970–74
Duckett, Forey (CB)	Nevada–Reno	1994
Dugans, Ron (WR)	Florida State	2000–02

Dunn, David (WR)	Fresno State	1995–98
Dunn, Paul (RB)	U.S. International	1970
Durko, Sandy (S)	Southern California	1970–72
Dyer, Ken (S)	Arizona State	1969–71
Eaddy, James (NT)	New York Tech	1987
Edmonds, Chris (TE)	West Virginia	2002–03
Edwards, Eddie (DE)	Miami (Florida)	1977–88
Elliott, Lenvil (RB)	NE Missouri State	1973–78
Ely, Larry (LB)	Iowa	1970–71
Elzey, Paul (LB)	Toledo	1968
Erickson, Bernard (LB)	Abilene Christian	1968
Ernst, Mike (QB)	Cal State–Fullerton	1973–74
Esiason, Boomer (QB)	Maryland	1984–92, 1997
Fain, Richard (CB)	Florida	1991
Fairchild, Greg (G)	Tulsa	1976–77
Fanene, Jonathan (DE)	Utah	2005–07
Farley, John (RB)	Cal State–Sacramento	1984
Farmer, Danny (WR)	UCLA	2000–02
Fears, Willie (DE)	Northwestern State (Louisiana)	1987
Fenner, Derrick (FB)	North Carolina	1992–94
Fest, Howard (G)	Texas	1968–75
Fisher, Charles (CB)	West Virginia	1999–2000
Fitzpatrick, Ryan (QB)	Harvard	2007
Flaherty, Tom (LB)	Northwestern	1987
Fletcher, John (G)	Texas A&I	1987
Foley, Steve (LB)	Northeast Louisiana	1998–2003
Fontenot, Jerry (C)	Texas A&M	2004
Ford, Mike (QB)	Southern Methodist	1982
Francis, James (LB)	Baylor	1990–98
Franklin, Pat (RB)	Southwest Texas State	1987
Frazier, Andre (LB)	Cincinnati	2006–07

Frazier, Curt (CB)	Fresno State	1968
Frazier, Guy (LB)	Wyoming	1981–84
Frerotte, Gus (QB)	Tulsa	2002
Frier, Mike (DE)	Appalachian State	1992–94
Frisch, David (TE)	Colorado State	1993–94
Fritts, Stan (RB)	North Carolina State	1975–76
Fulcher, David (S)	Arizona State	1986–92
Fulhage, Scott (P)	Kansas State	1987–88
Fuller, Mike (S)	Auburn	1981–82
Gallery, Jim (K)	Minnesota	1989
Garrett, John (WR)	Princeton	1989
Garrett, Shane (WR)	Texas A&M	1991–92
Gaynor, Doug (QB)	Cal State–Long Beach	1986
Geathers, Robert (DE)	Georgia	2004–07
Gehrke, Jack (WR)	Utah	1969
George, Tim (WR)	Carson-Newman	1973
Ghiaciuc, Eric (C)	Central Michigan	2005–07
Gibler, Andy (TE)	Missouri	1983
Gibson, Damon (WR)	Iowa	1998
Gibson, Oliver (DT)	Notre Dame	1999–2003
Gilliard, Cory (S)	Ball State	1997
Glass, Bill (G)	Baylor	1980
Glover, LaVar (CB)	Cincinnati	2002
Goff, Mike (G)	Iowa	1998–2003
Gordon, Alex (LB)	Cincinnati	1991–93
Graham, Kenny (S)	Washington State	1970
Graham, Scottie (RB)	Ohio State	1997
Graham, Shayne (K)	Virginia Tech	2003–07
Grant, Alan (CB)	Stanford	1993
Grant, David (NT)	West Virginia	1988–91
Granville, Billy (LB)	Duke	1997–2000
Graves, White (S)	Louisiana State	1968
Green, Dave (P)	Ohio U.	1974–75
Green, Harold (RB)	South Carolina	1990–95

Green, Skyler (WR)	Louisiana State	2007
Griffin, Archie (RB)	Ohio State	1976–83
Griffin, Damon (WR)	Oregon	1999–2000
Griffin, James (S)	Middle Tennessee State	1983–85
Griffin, Jim (DE)	Grambling	1968
Griffin, Ray (CB)	Ohio State	1978–84
Groce, Clif (FB)	Texas A&M	1999–2000
Guillory, John (S)	Stanford	1969–70
Gunn, Lance (S)	Texas	1993
Gunner, Harry (DE)	Oregon State	1968–69
Gutierrez, Brock (C)	Central Michigan	1996–2002
Haddix, Wayne (CB)	Liberty	1991
Haffner, Mike (WR)	UCLA	1971
Hall, Cory (S)	Fresno State	1999–2002
Hall, Leon (CB)	Michigan	2007
Hamilton, Lawrence (WR)	Stephen F. Austin	2003
Hammerstein, Mike (DE)	Michigan	1986–90
Hannula, Jim (T)	Northern Illinois	1983
Hardy, Adrian (CB)	Northwestern State (Louisiana)	1994–95
Hardy, Kevin (LB)	Illinois	2003–04
Hargrove, Jim (RB)	Wake Forest	1981
Harmon, Ed (LB)	Louisville	1969
Harris, Bo (LB)	Louisiana State	1975–82
Harris, Jim (CB)	Howard Payne	1971
Harris, M.L. (TE)	Kansas State	1980–85
Harris, Nick (P)	California	2001–03
Hawkins, Artrell (CB)	Cincinnati	1998–2003
Hayes, Jeff (P)	North Carolina	1986
Headrick, Sherrill (LB)	TCU	1968
Hearst, Garrison (RB)	Georgia	1996
Heath, Jo-Jo (KR)	Pittsburgh	1980
Heath, Rodney (CB)	Minnesota	1999–2001
Henry, Chris (WR)	West Virginia	2005–07
Henson, Champ (RB)	Ohio State	1975

Herock, Ken (TE)	West Virginia	1968
Herring, Kim (S)	Penn State	2004–05
Hertel, Rob (QB)	Southern California	1978
Hibler, Mike (LB)	Stanford	1968
Hicks, Bryan (S)	McNeese State	1980–84
Hill, Jeff (WR)	Purdue	1994–96
Hillary, Ira (WR)	South Carolina	1987–89
Hinkle, George (DE)	Arizona	1993
Holden, Steve (WR)	Arizona State	1977
Holifield, John (RB)	West Virginia	1988–89
Holland, Vernon (T)	Tennessee State	1971–79
Hollas, Don (QB)	Rice	1991–94
Holman, Rodney (TE)	Tulane	1982–92
Holt, Glenn (WR)	Kentucky	2007
Horn, Rod (NT)	Nebraska	1980–81
Horne, Greg (P)	Arkansas	1987
Horton, Ray (CB)	Washington	1983–88
Houshmandzadeh, T.J. (WR)	Oregon State	2001–07
Howard, Ty (CB)	Ohio State	1999
Howc, Garry (NT)	Colorado	1993
Hundon, James (WR)	Portland State	1996–99
Hunt, Bobby (S)	Auburn	1968–69
Hunt, Gary (CB)	Memphis State	1987
Hunt, Ron (T)	Oregon	1976–78
Inglis, Tim (LB)	Toledo	1987–88
Jackson, Bernard (S)	Washington State	1972–76
Jackson, Dexter (S)	Florida State	2006–07
Jackson, John (T)	Eastern Kentucky	2000–01
Jackson, LaDairis (LB)	Oregon State	2003–04
Jackson, Robert (S)	Central Michigan	1981–87, 1989
Jackson, Willie (WR)	Florida	1998–99
James, Lynn (WR)	Arizona State	1990–91

James, Tory (CB)	Louisiana State	2003–06
Jauron, Dick (S)	Yale	1978–81
Jeanty, Rashad (LB)	Central Florida	2006–07
Jefferson, Kevin (LB)	Lehigh	1994–95
Jeffries, Curtis (TE)	Louisville	1987
Jenkins, Mike (WR)	Hampton	1997
Jennings, Ligarius (CB)	Tennessee State	2001–02
Jennings, Stanford (RB)	Furman	1984–90
Jetton, Paul (C)	Texas	1989–91
Johnson, Bill (RB)	Arkansas State	1985–87
Johnson, Bob (C)	Tennessee	1968–79
Johnson, Chad (WR)	Oregon State	2001–07
Johnson, Donnell (T)	Johnson C. Smith	1993
Johnson, Doug (QB)	Florida	2006
Johnson, Essex (RB)	Grambling	1968–75
Johnson, Jeremi (FB)	Western Kentucky	2003–07
Johnson, Jim (CB)	South Carolina State	1969
Johnson, John (LB)	Clemson	1994
Johnson, Ken (DE)	Indiana	1971–77
Johnson, Landon (LB)	Purdue	2004–07
Johnson, Lee (P)	Brigham Young	1988–98
Johnson, Mark (S)	Western Kentucky	1987
Johnson, Pete (FB)	Ohio State	1977–83
Johnson, Riall (LB)	Stanford	2001–03
Johnson, Rudi (RB)	Auburn	2001–07
Johnson, Tim (DT)	Penn State	1996
Johnson, Walter (DT)	Los Angeles State	1977
Joiner, Charlie (WR)	Grambling	1972–75
Jolitz, Evan (LB)	Cincinnati	1974
Jones, Bob (S)	Virginia Union	1973–74
Jones, Dan (T)	Maine	1993–95
Jones, David (CB)	Wingate	2007
Jones, Dhani (LB)	Michigan	2007
Jones, Herana-Daze (S)	Indiana	2006–07
Jones, Levi (T)	Arizona State	2002–07

Jones, Rod (Roderick) (CB)	Southern Methodist	1990–96
Jones, Rod (Rodrek) (T)	Kansas	1996–2000
Jones, Roger (CB)	Tennessee State	1994–96
Jones, Scott (T)	Washington	1989, 1991
Jones, Willie Lee (DT)	Kansas State	1968–71
Jordan, Kevin (WR)	UCLA	1996
Joseph, James (RB)	Auburn	1995
Joseph, Johnathan (CB)	South Carolina	2006–07
Joseph, Kerry (QB)	McNeese State	1996
Justin, Paul (QB)	Arizona State	1998
Kaesviharn, Kevin (S)	Augustana (South Dakota)	2001–06
Kalis, Todd (G)	Arizona State	1995
Kattus, Eric (TE)	Michigan	1986–91
Kearney, Tim (LB)	Northern Michigan	1972–74
Keaton, Curtis (RB)	James Madison	2000–01
Keeling, Rex (P)	Samford	1968
Kellermann, Ernie (S)	Miami (Ohio)	1972
Kelly, Bob (T)	New Mexico State	1968
Kelly, Joe (LB)	Washington	1986–89
Kelly, Mike (TE)	Davidson	1970–72
Kelly, Reggie (TE)	Mississippi State	2003–07
Kelly, Todd (DE)	Tennessee	1995–96
Kemp, Bobby (S)	Cal State–Fullerton	1981–86
Kern, Don (TE)	Arizona State	1984–85
Kieft, Adam (T)	Central Michigan	2005–06
Kilmer, Ethan (S)	Penn State	2006
Kindricks, Bill (DT)	Alabama A&M	1968
King, Charlie (CB)	Purdue	1968–69
King, Emanuel (LB)	Alabama	1985–88
King, Joe (S)	Oklahoma State	1991
Kinnebrew, Larry (FB)	Tennessee State	1983–87
Kirk, Randy (LB)	San Diego State	1992–93
Kitna, Jon (QB)	Central Washington	2001–05
Klingler, David (QB)	Houston	1992–95

Koch, Pete (DT)	Maryland	1984
Koegel, Vic (LB)	Ohio State	1974
Kollar, Bill (DT)	Montana State	1974–76
Kooistra, Scott (G)	North Carolina State	2003–07
Kors, R.J. (S)	Cal State–Long Beach	1993
Kozerski, Bruce (G)	Holy Cross	1984–95
Kreider, Steve (WR)	Lehigh	1979–86
Krenzel, Craig (QB)	Ohio State	2005
Kresser, Eric (QB)	Marshall	1997–99
Krevis, Al (T)	Boston College	1975
Krumrie, Tim (NT)	Wisconsin	1983–94
Kurnick, Howie (LB)	Cincinnati	1979–80
Lamb, Ron (RB)	South Carolina	1968–71
Langford, Jevon (DE)	Oklahoma State	1996–2001
Lapham, Dave (G)	Syracuse	1974–83
Larson, Kyle (P)	Nebraska	2004–07
Law, Dennis (WR)	East Tennessee State	1978
Lawrie, Nate (TE)	Yale	2007
Lawson, Steve (G)	Kansas	1971–72
LeClair, Jim (LB)	North Dakota	1972–83
Leeuwenburg, Jay (G)	Colorado	1999
Levels, Dwayne (LB)	Oklahoma State	2003
Levenseller, Mike (WR)	Washington State	1979–80
Lewis, Dave (P)	Stanford	1970–73
Lewis, Marcus (DT)	Urbana	2006
Leyva, Victor (G)	Arizona State	2001–03
Linn, Jack (G)	West Virginia	1993
Livingston, Dale (P)	Western Michigan	1968–69
Logan, James (LB)	Memphis	1995
Logan, Marc (RB)	Kentucky	1987–88
Lott, Anthone (CB)	Florida	1997
Luchey, Nicolas (formerly Nick Williams) (FB)	Miami (Florida)	1999–2002, 2005
Lusby, Vaughn (CB)	Arkansas	1979

Lynch, James (FB)	Maryland	2004
Mack, Tremain (S)	Miami (Florida)	1997–2000
Maddox, Bob (DE)	Frostburg State	1974
Maidlow, Steve (LB)	Michigan State	1983–84
Manca, Massimo (K)	Penn State	1987
Manning, Aaron (CB)	Iowa State	1987
Manning, Roy (LB)	Michigan	2007
Manos, Sam (C)	Marshall	1987
Manual, Marquand (S)	Florida	2002–03
Marshall, Ed (WR)	Cameron (Oklahoma)	1971
Marshall, Lemar (LB)	Michigan State	2007
Martin, Mike (WR)	Illinois	1983–89
Martin, Terrance (DT)	North Carolina State	2004
Mathias, Ric (CB)	Wisconsin–LaCrosse	1998–99
Matlock, John (C)	Miami (Florida)	1968
Matson, Pat (G)	Oregon	1968–74
Matthews, Shane (QB)	Florida	2003
Maxey, Curtis (NT)	Grambling	1988
Maxwell, Jim (LB)	Gardner-Webb	2007
Maxwell, Marcus (WR)	Oregon	2007
Mayes, Rufus (T)	Ohio State	1970–78
Mays, Corey (LB)	Notre Dame	2007
McCall, Ed (WR)	Miles College	1968
McClendon, Skip (DE)	Arizona State	1987–91
McClure, Wayne (LB)	Mississippi	1968, 1970
McCluskey, David (RB)	Georgia	1987
McDaniel, John (WR)	Lincoln	1974–77
McDonald, Ricardo (LB)	Pittsburgh	1992–97
McGee, Tim (WR)	Tennessee	1986–92, 1994–95
McGee, Tony (TE)	Michigan	1993–2001
McGhee, Kanavis (LB)	Colorado	1994
McGill, Karmeeleyah (LB)	Notre Dame	1993
McInally, Pat (P)	Harvard	1976–85

McMullen, Kirk (TE)	Pittsburgh	2001
McNeal, Reggie (WR)	Texas A&M	2006
McVea, Warren (WR)	Houston	1968
Meehan, Greg (WR)	Bowling Green	1987
Megna, Marc (LB)	Richmond	2000
Melander, Jon (G)	Minnesota	1992
Melontree, Andrew (LB)	Baylor	1980
Middendorf, Dave (G)	Washington State	1968–69
Miles, Ostell (RB)	Houston	1992–93
Miller, Caleb (LB)	Arkansas	2004–07
Milne, Brian (FB)	Penn State	1996–99
Mitchell, Anthony (S)	Tuskegee	2004–06
Mitchell, Mack (DE)	Houston	1979
Mitchell, Scott (QB)	Utah	2000–01
Mitz, Alonzo (DE)	Florida	1991–92
Monds, Mario (DT)	Cincinnati	2001–02
Montgomery, Cleotha (RB)	Abilene Christian	1980
Montoya, Max (G)	UCLA	1979–89
Moore, Blake (C)	Wooster	1980–83
Moore, Eric (T)	Indiana	1994
Moore, Kelvin (S)	Morgan State	1998–99
Moore, Langston (DT)	South Carolina	2004
Moore, Larry (G)	Brigham Young	2004–05
Moore, Maulty (DT)	Bethune-Cookman	1975
Morabito, Tim (DT)	Boston College	1996
Morgan, Melvin (CB)	Mississippi Valley State	1976–78
Morrison, Reece (RB)	Southwest Texas State	1972–73
Moyer, Ken (G)	Toledo	1989–94
Muhlmann, Horst (K)	none	1969–74
Muñoz, Anthony (T)	Southern California	1980–92
Myers, Chip (WR)	Northwestern Oklahoma	1969–76
Myers, Greg (S)	Colorado State	1996–99
Myers, Michael (DT)	Alabama	2007
Myles, Reggie (CB)	Alabama	2002–05

Navies, Hannibal (LB)	Colorado	2005
Ndukwe, Chinedum (S)	Notre Dame	2007
Neal, Lorenzo (FB)	Fresno State	2001–02
Neal, Randy (LB)	Virginia	1995–96
Neidert, John (LB)	Louisville	1968
Nicholson, A.J. (LB)	Florida State	2006
Niehoff, Rob (S)	Cincinnati	1987
Nix, Roosevelt (DE)	Central State (Ohio)	1992–93
Norseth, Mike (QB)	Kansas	1987–88
Novak, Jack (TE)	Wisconsin	1975
O'Neal, Deltha (CB)	California	2004–07
O'Donnell, Neil (QB)	Maryland	1998
O'Dwyer, Matt (G)	Northwestern	1999–2003
Obrovac, Mike (G)	Bowling Green	1981–83
Ogbogu, Eric (DE)	Maryland	2002
Oglesby, Alfred (DT)	Houston	1995
Ogletree, Craig (LB)	Auburn	1990
Ohalete, Ifeanyi (S)	Southern California	2005
Oliver, Louis (S)	Florida	1994
Orlando, Bo (S)	West Virginia	1996–97
Palmer, Carson (QB)	Southern California	2003–07
Park, Ernie (G)	McMurry	1969
Parker, Carl (WR)	Vanderbilt	1988–89
Parker, Sirr (CB)	Texas A&M	2000
Parrish, Lemar (CB)	Lincoln	1970–77
Parten, Ty (DE)	Arizona	1993–95
Patterson, Elton (DE)	Central Florida	2003–04
Paul, Tito (CB)	Ohio State	1997
Payne, Rod (C)	Michigan	1997–98
Peacock, Elvis (RB)	Oklahoma	1981
Peko, Domata (DT)	Michigan State	2007
Pelfrey, Doug (K)	Kentucky	1993–99
Perreault, Pete (G)	Boston U.	1968

Perry, Chris (RB)	Michigan	2004–06
Perry, Jason (S)	North Carolina State	2002
Perry, Scott (CB)	Williams	1976–79
Perry, Tab (WR)	UCLA	2005–07
Peters, Frank (T)	Ohio U.	1969
Peterson, Ben (LB)	Pittsburgh State	1999
Peterson, Bill (LB)	San Jose State	1968–72
Philcox, Todd (QB)	Syracuse	1990
Phillips, Jess (RB)	Michigan State	1968–72
Phillips, Ray (LB)	Nebraska	1977–78
Pickens, Carl (WR)	Tennessee	1992–99
Pickering, Clay (WR)	Maine	1984–85
Pillman, Brian (LB)	Miami (Ohio)	1984
Pleasant, Marquis (WR)	Southern Methodist	1987
Poe, Bill (G)	Morehead State	1987
Pollack, David (LB)	Georgia	2005–06
Pollard, Trent (G)	Eastern Washington	1994–96
Poole, Nathan (RB)	Louisville	1979–80
Pope, Daniel (P)	Alabama	2000
Powell, Carl (DE)	Louisville	2003–05
Price, Mitchell (CB)	Tulane	1990–93
Pritchard, Ron (LB)	Arizona State	1972–77
Pureifory, Dave (DT)	Eastern Michigan	1978
Purvis, Andre (DT)	North Carolina	1997–99
Query, Jeff (WR)	Millikin	1992–95
Rackers, Neil (K)	Illinois	2000–02
Randall, Dennis (DE)	Oklahoma State	1968
Randolph, Al (CB)	Iowa	1972
Randolph, Thomas (CB)	Kansas State	1998
Ratliff, Keiwan (CB)	Florida	2004–07
Rayam, Tom (G)	Alabama	1992–93
Razzano, Rick (LB)	Virginia Tech	1980–84
Reasons, Gary (LB)	Northwestern State (Louisiana)	1992

Reaves, John (QB)	Florida	1975–78
Rehberg, Scott (G)	Central Michigan	2000–03
Reid, Mike (DT)	Penn State	1970–74
Reimers, Bruce (G)	Iowa State	1984–91
Reinke, Jeff (DE)	Mankato State	1987
Rembert, Reggie (WR)	West Virginia	1991–93
Rice, Andy (DT)	Texas Southern	1968–69
Rice, Dan (RB)	Michigan	1987
Richardson, Kyle (P)	Arkansas State	2003–04
Richey, Tom (G)	Kentucky	1987
Ridgle, Elston (DE)	Nevada–Reno	1992
Riggs, Jim (TE)	Clemson	1987–92
Riley, Bob (TE)	Indiana	1987
Riley, Ken (CB)	Florida A&M	1969–83
Rimington, Dave (C)	Nebraska	1983–87
Roberts, Terrell (CB)	Oregon State	2003–05
Robinson, Bryan (DT)	Fresno State	2005–07
Robinson, Frank (CB)	Boise State	1992
Robinson, Patrick (WR)	Tennessee State	1993
Robinson, Paul (RB)	Arizona	1968–72
Rogers, Lamar (DE)	Auburn	1991–92
Roman, Mark (CB)	Louisiana State	2000–03
Roman, Nick (DE)	Ohio State	1970–71
Romasko, Dave (TE)	Carroll College	1987
Romer, Rich (LB)	Union (New York)	1988–89
Ross, Adrian (LB)	Colorado State	1998–2003
Ross, Dan (TE)	Northeastern	1979–83, 1985
Rourke, Jim (G)	Boston College	1988
Rowe, Jeff (QB)	Nevada	2007
Rucker, Frostee (DE)	Southern California	2006–07
Rucker, Keith (DT)	Ohio Wesleyan	1994–95
Russell, Cliff (WR)	Utah	2004
Russell, Wade (TE)	Taylor	1987
Ruud, Tom (LB)	Nebraska	1978–79

Saddler, Rod (DE)	Texas A&M	1991
Sadowski, Troy (TE)	Georgia	1994–96
Saffold, Saint (WR)	San Jose State	1968
Santucci, Dan (C)	Notre Dame	2007
Sargent, Kevin (T)	Eastern Washington	1992–98
Savage, Tony (DE)	Washington State	1992
Sawyer, Corey (CB)	Florida State	1994–98
Sawyer, Ken (S)	Syracuse	1974
Schlegel, Anthony (LB)	Ohio State	2007
Schobel, Matt (TE)	TCU	2002–05
Schonert, Turk (QB)	Stanford	1980–85, 1987–89
Schroeder, Jay (QB)	UCLA	1993
Schuh, Jeff (LB)	Minnesota	1981–85
Schutt, Scott (LB)	North Dakota State	1987
Scott, Bill (CB)	Idaho	1968
Scott, Darnay (WR)	San Diego State	1994–2001
Scott, Greg (DT)	Hampton	2004
Scott, Tom (T)	East Carolina	1993
Scrafford, Kirk (T)	Montana	1990–92
Sellers, Lance (LB)	Boise State	1987
Shade, Sam (S)	Alabama	1995–98
Shaw, Eric (LB)	Louisiana Tech	1992–94
Shaw, Scott (C)	Michigan State	1998
Shaw, Sedrick (RB)	Iowa	1999
Shelby, Willie (RB)	Alabama	1976–77
Shelling, Chris (S)	Auburn	1995–96
Sherman, Rod (WR)	Southern California	1968
Shinners, John (G)	Xavier (Ohio)	1973–77
Shumon, Ron (LB)	Wichita State	1978
Simmons, Brian (LB)	North Carolina	1998–2006
Simmons, Clyde (DE)	Western Carolina	1998
Simmons, John (CB)	Southern Methodist	1981–86
Simmons, Marcello (CB)	Southern Methodist	1993

Simpkins, Ron (LB)	Michigan	1980–86
Sims, Reggie (TE)	Northern Illinois	1987
Skow, Jim (DE)	Nebraska	1986–89
Smiley, Tom (RB)	Lamar	1968
Smith, Akili (QB)	Oregon	1999–2002
Smith, Artie (DE)	Louisiana Tech	1994–96
Smith, Brad (LB)	TCU	1993
Smith, Daryl (CB)	North Alabama	1987–88
Smith, Dave (T)	Southern Illinois	1988
Smith, Fletcher (CB)	Tennessee State	1968–71
Smith, Gary (G)	Virginia Tech	1984
Smith, Jeff (DE)	Earlham College	1987
Smith, Justin (DE)	Missouri	2001–07
Smith, Ken (G)	Miami (Ohio)	1987
Smith, Kendal (WR)	Utah State	1989–90
Smith, Ron (DT)	Lane College	2002
Smith, Shaun (DT)	South Carolina	2004–06
Smith, Tommie (WR)	San Jose State	1969
Spearman, Armegis (LB)	Mississippi	2000–02
Spencer, Jimmy (CB)	Florida	1996–97
Spikes, Takeo (LB)	Auburn	1998–2002
Spiller, Phil (S)	Los Angeles State	1968
Sprotte, Jimmy (LB)	Arizona	1998–99
St. Clair, Mike (DE)	Grambling	1980–82
St. Louis, Brad (LS)	SW Missouri State	2000–07
Staley, Bill (DT)	Utah	1968–69
Stallings, Ramondo (DE)	San Diego State	1994–98
Steele, Glen (DT)	Michigan	1998–2003
Stegall, Milt (WR)	Miami (Ohio)	1992–94
Steinbach, Eric (G)	Iowa	2003–06
Stepanovich, Alex (C)	Ohio State	2007
Stephens, Jamain (T)	North Carolina A&T	1999–2002
Stephens, Santo (LB)	Temple	1994
Stevens, Larry (LB)	Michigan	2004–05
Stewart, Tony (TE)	Penn State	2002–06

Stofa, John (QB)	Buffalo	1968–69
Stubbs, Daniel (DE)	Miami (Florida)	1991–93
Suggs, Shafer (S)	Ball State	1980
Sulfsted, Alex (T)	Miami (Ohio)	2004
Sunter, Ian (K)	none	1980
Swanson, Terry (P)	Massachusetts	1968–69
Szalay, Thatcher (G)	Montana	2002–03
Tamm, Ralph (G)	West Chester	1991
Tate, Rodney (RB)	Texas	1982–83
Taylor, Craig (RB)	West Virginia	1989–91
Terry, Tim (LB)	Temple	1997
Thomas, Eric (CB)	Tulane	1987–92
Thomas, Lee (DE)	Jackson State	1973
Thomas, Sean (CB)	TCU	1985
Thomas, Speedy (WR)	Utah	1969–72
Thomason, Jeff (TE)	Oregon	1992–93
Thompson, Craig (TE)	North Carolina A&T	1992–93
Thompson, Jack (QB)	Washington State	1979–82
Thompson, Lamont (S)	Washington State	2002–03
Thompson, Mike (NT)	Wisconsin	1998
Thornton, John (DT)	West Virginia	2002–07
Thornton, Reggie (WR)	Bowling Green	1993
Thurman, Odell (LB)	Georgia	2005
Tigges, Mark (T)	Western Illinois	1987
Tovar, Steve (LB)	Ohio State	1993–97
Townsend, Brian (LB)	Michigan	1992
Truitt, Greg (LS)	Penn State	1994–99
Trumpy, Bob (TE)	Utah	1968–77
Tuatagaloa, Natu (DE)	California	1989–91
Tumulty, Tom (LB)	Pittsburgh	1996–99
Turner, Clem (RB)	Cincinnati	1969
Turner, Deacon (RB)	San Diego State	1978–80
Turner, Jimmy (CB)	UCLA	1983–86
Tuten, Melvin (T)	Syracuse	1995–96

Tweet, Rodney (WR)	South Dakota	1987
Twyner, Gunnard (WR)	Western Illinois	1997
Verser, David (WR)	Kansas	1981–84
Vieira, Steven (G)	UCLA	2005
Vincent, Ted (DT)	Wichita State	1978
Vinson, Fernandus (S)	North Carolina State	1991–94
Vitiello, Sandro (K)	Massachusetts	1980
Von Oelhoffen, Kimo (DT)	Boise State	1994–99
Wagner, Ray (T)	Kent State	1982
Walker, Bracey (S)	North Carolina	1994–96
Walker, Kevin (LB)	Maryland	1988–92
Walker, Rick (TE)	UCLA	1977–79
Wallerstedt, Brett (LB)	Arizona State	1994–96
Walsh, John (QB)	Brigham Young	1995
Walter, Dave (QB)	Michigan Tech	1987
Walter, Joe (T)	Texas Tech	1985–97
Walter, Kevin (WR)	Eastern Michigan	2003–05
Walters, Stan (T)	Syracuse	1972–74
Ward, David (LB)	Southern Arkansas	1987
Ware, Derek (TE)	Central State (Oklahoma)	1995
Warren, Dewey (QB)	Tennessee	1968
Warrick, Peter (WR)	Florida State	2000–04
Washington, Kelley (WR)	Tennessee	2003–06
Washington, Sam (CB)	Mississippi Valley State	1985
Washington, Ted (RB)	San Diego State	1968
Watson, Kenny (RB)	Penn State	2003–07
Watson, Pete (RB)	Tufts	1972
Weathersby, Dennis (CB)	Oregon State	2003–04
Weaver, Emanuel (NT)	South Carolina	1982–83
Webb, Richmond (T)	Texas A&M	2001–02
Webster, Nate (LB)	Miami (Florida)	2004–05
Wells, Dana (NT)	Arizona	1989
Wells, Mike (QB)	Illinois	1977

Westbrook, Michael (WR)	Colorado	2002
Wheeler, Leonard (CB)	Troy State	1992–96
White, Andre (TE)	Florida A&M	1968
White, Leon (LB)	Brigham Young	1986–91
White, Marvin (S)	Texas Christian	2007
White, Mike (DT)	Albany State (Ga.)	1979–80
White, Sheldon (CB)	Miami (Ohio)	1993
White, Sherman (DE)	California	1972–75
Whitehead, Terrence (RB)	Oregon	2006
Whiteside, Keyon (LB)	Tennessee	2003
Whitley, Wilson (DT)	Houston	1977–82
Whitten, Bobby (T)	Kansas	1981
Whittington, Bernard (DT)	Indiana	2001–02
Whitworth, Andrew (G)	Louisiana State	2006–07
Wilcots, Solomon (S)	Colorado	1987–90
Wilhelm, Erik (QB)	Oregon State	1989–91, 1993-97
Wilkerson, Ben (C)	Louisiana State	2006
Wilkins, Marcus (LB)	Texas	2004–06
Wilkinson, Dan (DT)	Ohio State	1994–97
Williams, Alfred (LB)	Colorado	1991–94
Williams, Bobbie (G)	Arkansas	2004–07
Williams, Darryl (S)	Miami (Florida)	1992–95, 2000–01
Williams, Ed (RB)	Langston	1974–75
Williams, Gary (WR)	Ohio State	1984
Williams, Jim (DB)	Alcorn State	1969
Williams, Madieu (S)	Maryland	2004–07
Williams, Monk (WR)	Arkansas A,M&N	1968
Williams, Nick (changed name to Nicolas Luchey) (FB)	Miami (Florida)	1999–2002, 2005
Williams, Reggie (LB)	Dartmouth	1976–89
Williams, Stepfret (WR)	Northeast Louisiana	1998
Williams, Tony (DT)	Memphis	2001–04

Willis, Fred (RB)	Boston College	1971–72
Wilson, Joe (RB)	Holy Cross	1973
Wilson, Mike (RB)	Dayton	1969–70
Wilson, Mike (T)	Georgia	1978–85
Wilson, Quincy (RB)	West Virginia	2006–07
Wilson, Reinard (LB)	Florida State	1997–2002
Wilson, Stanley (RB)	Oklahoma	1983–84, 1986, 1988
Winans, Tydus (WR)	Fresno State	1996
Withycombe, Mike (T)	Fresno State	1991–92
Woods, Ickey (FB)	Nevada–Las Vegas	1988–91
Wright, Dana (RB)	Findlay	1987
Wright, Ernie (T)	Ohio State	1968–71
Wright, Lawrence (S)	Florida	1997–99
Wyche, Sam (QB)	Furman	1968–70
Yeast, Craig (WR)	Kentucky	1999–2000
Zander, Carl (LB)	Tennessee	1985–91
Zellars, Ray (FB)	Notre Dame	1998

Page 2: The Bengals introduced their striped helmets in 1981.

Page 13: Dick LeBeau appeared in the 1970 movie *Too Late the Hero* as Michael Caine's double.

Page 20: Twice—in the regular-season opener against Denver on September 7, 2003, and in the regular-season finale against Cleveland on December 28, 2003. The Bengals lost both those games and never wore those exact same pants again.

Page 27: Sam Wyche scored on a five-yard run with 13:08 left in the first quarter of a 31–21 victory over Oakland on September 20, 1970.

Page 29: Pittsburgh Steelers coach Bill Cowher asked his players "Who dey?" after Pittsburgh won at Cincinnati, 31–17, on January 8, 2006. The players answered, "We dey." Cowher "borrowed" it again at a rally in Pittsburgh after the Steelers won the Super Bowl. This time he modified it to, "Who dey? Who dey? Who dey? Who dey think gonna beat the NFL? Pittsburgh Steelers, world champs!"

Page 40: Rashaan Salaam of Colorado, another junior running back, won the 1994 Heisman Trophy.

Page 48: Forrest Gregg's full name is Alvis Forrest Gregg.

Page 65: A carpenter. He builds furniture in the workshop he has at his home.

Page 69: Lemar Parrish returned two interceptions for touchdowns against Houston on December 17, 1972.

Page 73: The only other Bengals player besides quarterback Ken Anderson to be named the NFL's Most Valuable Player was quarterback Boomer Esiason, in 1988.

Page 77: The other former Bengals player who joined Dave Lapham when he jumped to the USFL's New Jersey Generals was linebacker Jim LeClair.

Page 81: Running back Tom Smiley wore No. 45 in 1968.

Page 88: Doug Pelfrey, the Bengals kicker from 1993 to 1999, is the team's second-leading scorer, with 660 points.

Page 91: Anthony Cris Collinsworth.

Page 97: Anthony Muñoz was a pitcher on USC's NCAA championship baseball team in 1978.

Page 105: Krumrie wrestled in 1979 and 1980, finishing fifth in the Big Ten as a sophomore.

Page 108: Boomer Esiason's real first name is Norman.

Page 111: Ickey Woods's real first name is Elbert.

Page 117: Rickey Dixon was the Bengals' starting free safety in 1989.

Page 123: Larry Kinnebrew and Corey Dillon each scored 24 points with four touchdowns in a single game. Kinnebrew did it October 28, 1984, at Houston, and Dillon did it December 4, 1997, against Tennessee.

Page 131: Ken Anderson set records for completions, with 25, and completion percentage, with 73.5 percent. Both of them have since been surpassed.

Page 136: Three Bengals started in the same positions in Super Bowl XVI and XXIII—left tackle Anthony Muñoz, right guard Max Montoya, and right outside linebacker Reggie Williams.

Page 144: Keyshawn Johnson and Samari Rolle.

Page 149: Rob Johnson, who started one game in 1991, was the first true freshman to start at quarterback for Southern Cal.

Page 155: Rudi Johnson's full name is Berudi Ali Johnson. In Swahili, Berudi means "cool." His middle name is in honor of boxer Muhammad Ali.

Notes

Pro Football in Cincinnati

"Those final two victories were big moments…" Brown, Paul, with Jack Clary. *PB: The Paul Brown Story*. New York: Atheneum, 1979, page 310.

The Father of the Franchise

"I simply felt that it was the proper time to step down…." Brown, Paul, with Jack Clary. *PB: The Paul Brown Story*. New York: Atheneum, 1979, page 3.

"My basic philosophy…" Brown, Paul, with Jack Clary. *PB: The Paul Brown Story*. New York: Atheneum, 1979, page 5.

"I have not regretted the decision…" Brown, Paul, with Jack Clary. *PB: The Paul Brown Story*. New York: Atheneum, 1979, page 338.

The Field Generals

"I felt he shared my general coaching beliefs…" Brown, Paul, with Jack Clary. *PB: The Paul Brown Story*. New York: Atheneum, 1979, page 337.

"Homer has done a superlative job…" Brown, Paul, with Jack Clary. *PB: The Paul Brown Story*. New York: Atheneum, 1979, page 337.

Clothes Make the Men

"I was also involved in designing our uniforms…" Brown, Paul, with Jack Clary. *PB: The Paul Brown Story*. New York: Atheneum, 1979, page 301–2.

Home Sweet Home

"The two seasons we spent at Nippert were fun.…" Brown, Paul, with Jack Clary. *PB: The Paul Brown Story*. New York: Atheneum, 1979, pages 299–300.

The Rallying Cry

"Who dey?" Curnutte, Mark. "Who dey? Cowher, dat's who," *The Cincinnati Enquirer*, September 21, 2006.

"Some teams have a certain tradition…" Kelly, Kevin. "Who dey! It's back, but where'd it come from?" *The Cincinnati Enquirer*, October 2, 2005.

"I picked it up as soon as I got here…" Kelly, Kevin. "Who dey! It's back, but where'd it come from?" *The Cincinnati Enquirer*, October 2, 2005.

"I can confirm that this kind of chant…" Kelly, Kevin. "Who dey! It's back, but where'd it come from?" *The Cincinnati Enquirer*, October 2, 2005.

"It's about an Irish bar…" Sloat, Bill. "Bengals fans get 'Who Dey' in sun; saying wilted after 15 years of futility; now it's reemerged with a vengeance," *The* (Cleveland) *Plain Dealer*, January 6, 2006.

Bonus Babies and Bombs

"Ken ranks behind Otto Graham…" Brown, Paul, with Jack Clary. *PB: The Paul Brown Story*. New York: Atheneum, 1979, page 326.

"Isaac has since become one of the great stars of our era…" Brown, Paul, with Jack Clary. *PB: The Paul Brown Story*. New York: Atheneum, 1979, page 331.

"A few people were surpriscd…" Brown, Paul, with Jack Clary. *PB: The Paul Brown Story*. New York: Atheneum, 1979, page 305.

"We felt, however, that he was basically a good person…" Brown, Paul, with Jack Clary. *PB: The Paul Brown Story*. New York: Atheneum, 1979, page 306.

A Most Colorful Coach

"That operation changed my life…" Iacobelli, Pete. "High school rejuvenates Sam Wyche," *The* (Cleveland) *Plain Dealer*, July 27, 2006.

A No-Nonsense Coach

"Yes, by far…" Curnutte, Mark. "These guys have a long road," *The Cincinnati Enquirer*, July 25, 2006.

"But it really doesn't matter…" Curnutte, Mark. "These guys have a long road," *The Cincinnati Enquirer*, July 25, 2006.

"To do what he did…" Attner, Paul. "Wrestling with wildcats; Marvin Lewis earned his coaching stripes quickly by turning the Bengals from a punch line into a playoff team. But his players' lawlessness threatens to tarnish his turnaround job." *The Sporting News*, November 3, 2006.

"Marvin has done a wonderful job…" Curnutte, Mark. "Lewis's deal extended again," *The Cincinnati Enquirer*, February 17, 2006.

"My father [Paul Brown] coached…" Curnutte, Mark. "Lewis's deal extended again," *The Cincinnati Enquirer*, February 17, 2006.

The Bengals' Best Quarterback?

"Ken Anderson ranks just behind Otto Graham…" Brown, Paul, with Jack Clary. *PB: The Paul Brown Story*. New York: Atheneum, 1979, page 326.

"If there was any gamble…" Brown, Paul, with Jack Clary. *PB: The Paul Brown Story*. New York: Atheneum, 1979, page 326.

"Kenny, first of all, is a good person…." Ludwig, Chick. "Anderson saw it coming; former Bengals QB talked up Cincinnati to number one pick Palmer." *Dayton Daily News*, October 9, 2005.

"He got real emotional…." Ludwig, Chick. "Anderson saw it coming; former Bengals QB talked up Cincinnati to number one pick Palmer." *Dayton Daily News*, October 9, 2005.

"People were concerned about him…" Ludwig, Chick. "Anderson saw it coming; former Bengals QB talked up Cincinnati to number one pick Palmer." *Dayton Daily News*, October 9, 2005.

The Epitome of Toughness

"I coach in the grass," Whitlock, Jason. "Krumrie's intensity valuable," *The Kansas City Star*, August 4, 2006.

"I just have to be consistent…" Whitlock, Jason. "Krumrie's intensity valuable," *The Kansas City Star*, August 4, 2006.

The Bengals' Other Quarterback

"After Jimmy kicked that…" Grossi, Tony. "A Taylor-made victory; Montana TD pass clincher," *The* (Cleveland) *Plain Dealer*, January 23, 1989.

"I think that what…" Grossi, Tony. "A Taylor-made victory; Montana TD pass clincher," *The* (Cleveland) *Plain Dealer*, January 23, 1989.

Ten Great Games

"When I ran off the field…" Brown, Paul, with Jack Clary. *PB: The Paul Brown Story*. New York: Atheneum, 1979, page 324.

"He was unreal," Heaton, Chuck. "Browns await Bengals' aerial circus," *The* (Cleveland) *Plain Dealer*, November 19, 1975.

"He's cool, efficient, the best…" Heaton, Chuck. "Browns await Bengals' aerial circus," *The* (Cleveland) *Plain Dealer*, November 19, 1975.

"I told them that there was nothing we could do…" Heaton, Chuck. "Super Bowl XVI: Bengals versus 49ers, Chargers chilled by Cincy," *The* (Cleveland) *Plain Dealer*, January 11, 1982.

"It was very, very windy…" Heaton, Chuck. "Super Bowl XVI: Bengals versus 49ers, Chargers chilled by Cincy," *The* (Cleveland) *Plain Dealer*, January 11, 1982.

"I don't like their team…" Hooley, Bruce. "Wyche takes delight in 61–7 rout of Oilers," *The* (Cleveland) *Plain Dealer*, December 18, 1989.

"Our job is to stop them…" Hooley, Bruce. "Wyche takes delight in 61–7 rout of Oilers," *The* (Cleveland) *Plain Dealer*, December 18, 1989.

"From the time we started…" Prisco, Pete. "Guarantees aside, Bengals are serious contender," CBS Sportsline, cbs.sportsline.com, November 16, 2003.

The 1981 Super Bowl Season

"I don't see how anybody can boo him now," From wire reports. "Cincinnati takes lead in Central," *The* (Cleveland) *Plain Dealer*, September 28, 1981.

"What have I played, 12 years?" From wire reports. "Cincy first as Steelers, Oilers fall," *The* (Cleveland) *Plain Dealer*, October 19, 1981.

"This game was settled on the first drive," Associated Press. "Aggressive Saints jolt Bengals, 17–7," *The* (Cleveland) *Plain Dealer*, October 26, 1981.

"He's like a heat-seeking missile," From wire reports. "Bengals rout Oilers, 49ers nip Steelers in AFC Central," *The* (Cleveland) *Plain Dealer*, November 2, 1981.

"You don't win many football games…" Heaton, Chuck. "Bengals' playoff march is stalled by 49ers, 21–3," *Cleveland Plain Dealer*, December 7, 1981.

"He was just the right man for us," Heaton, Chuck. "Anderson leads Bengals to title," *The* (Cleveland) *Plain Dealer*, November 14, 1981.

"I wish you all could experience…" Heaton, Chuck. "Anderson: 'This is simply great,'" *The* (Cleveland) *Plain Dealer*, November 14, 1981.

"Anderson was outstanding…" Schneider, Russell. "Bengals win as error kills Bills," *The* (Cleveland) *Plain Dealer*, January 4, 1982.

"Joe Montana did a superb job…" Schneider, Russell. "49ers are Super champs," *The* (Cleveland) *Plain Dealer*, January 25, 1982.

"We were loose all week…" Heaton, Chuck. "Bengals come up short playing catch-up," *The* (Cleveland) *Plain Dealer*, January 25, 1982.

The 1988 Super Bowl Season

"If you do what you're supposed to do…" Associated Press. "Bengals rally wins," *The* (Cleveland) *Plain Dealer*, September 12, 1988.

"We did a lot of things early…" Hooley, Bruce. "Bengals overcome errors, whip Jets," *The* (Cleveland) *Plain Dealer*, October 10, 1988.

"The worst exhibition of football…" Heaton, Chuck. "Boomer on mark, leads rout by Bengals," *The* (Cleveland) *Plain Dealer*, November 7, 1988.

"We played probably one of the best…" Associated Press. "Last-second losers Chiefs rally jolts Bengals," *The* (Cleveland) *Plain Dealer*, November 14, 1988.

"This is by far and away the best…" Associated Press. "Bengals offense wins," *The* (Cleveland) *Plain Dealer*, November 28, 1988.

"Eddie DeBartolo, Coach Bill Walsh…" Zimmerman, Paul. "Joe Cool: the 49ers' Joe Montana knocked the Bengals cold with a spectacular late rally in the Super Bowl," *Sports Illustrated*, January 30, 1989.

Chad Johnson: Talking a Good Game

"I didn't want to go somewhere they were already winning…" Daugherty, Paul. *Chad: I Can't Be Stopped*. Wilmington, Ohio: Orange Frazer Press, 2006.

NFL Quarterback and Regular Guy

"I'm amazed, really…" Starkey, Joe. "Calm, cool Palmer has burning desire to win," *Pittsburgh Tribune Review*, September 24, 2006.

The Quiet Johnson

"I don't know…" Cabot, Mary Kay. "Rudi awakening for Browns again," *The* (Cleveland) *Plain Dealer*, December 12, 2005.

"You can't really appreciate…" Ludwig, Chick. "Johnson hits jackpot with Bengals; running back gets $26 million contract for five years," *Dayton Daily News*, March 17, 2005.

"You pick your poison…" Cabot, Mary Kay. "Bengals offense looks up to stars," *The* (Cleveland) *Plain Dealer*, November 26, 2006.

"It's fun sitting back there…" Wise, John P. "Rudi's rampage keeps Bengals upbeat; Johnson's best day gives him 1,000 reasons to smile," *The* (Cleveland) *Plain Dealer*, November 29, 2004.